PARADISE
ON EARTH

PARADISE
ON EARTH

First published 1995,

© JIDD Publishers

Harper-MacRae & Associates Inc.

1716 Canvasback Lane

Columbus, OH 43215. USA

Managing Editor: Mark Swadling

Design: BPD Graphic Associates, Canberra, ACT.

Writing: Tim Baker, Linda Newton, Mark Swadling and
Jinki Trevillian.

Project Co-ordination: Kay Osborne, Robert Osborne,
Tony Duffy, John Burke (IUCN).

Editorial Consultants: IUCN: Jim Thorsell, Senior Advisor
Natural Heritage, Jeffrey McNeely, Chief Conservation
Officer; World Conservation Monitoring Center (WCMC).

Concept: Robert Osborne and Mark Swadling

Pre-press Production: Fancy Graphic Production, Hong Kong

Telephone (852) 793 2263

Facsimile (852) 793 2048

Printed and Bound : Inter Scan Limited , Hong Kong

National Library of Australia Cataloguing-in-Publication data:

JIDD Publishers

Paradise on Earth

Includes Index

ISBN 0-646-19397-X

Produced by Harper-MacRae Publishing Pty Limited
for JIDD Publishers

6–8 Patonga Drive

Patonga 2256 Australia

Telephone 61-(0) 2 660 4400

Facsimile 61-(0) 2 660 4188

Printed on acid free paper produced from new growth
plantation forest.

(PAGE ONE) *Part of Australia's East Coast Temperate Rainforests.*

(PREVIOUS PAGE) *African fish eagle, Lake Malawi.*

(THIS PAGE) *Ocelot.*

CONTENTS

PREFACE

'The Aboriginals had an earthbound philosophy. The earth gave life to a man; gave him his food, language and intelligence; and the earth took him back when he died. A man's 'own country', even an empty stretch of spinifex, was itself a sacred ikon that must remain unscarred.'

- Bruce Chatwin, 'The Songlines'

Such a relationship between people and their land is largely absent from the world today. To find it we need to search amongst the few indigenous cultures which have survived into modern times - cultures such as those of the remaining Australian and American aboriginal tribes. Cultures which hold strong attachments to their environment, and so have been able to pass on to future generations a wealth of natural heritage.

Sadly, this heritage is endangered. The World Heritage Convention was adopted in 1972 at the instigation of the United States of America, so that the world's remaining places of outstanding universal significance would be protected for all time through international co-operation. Today there are over 400 sites from almost 100 countries on the World Heritage List. The approved natural sites, the subject of this superb publication, represent the inspirational and irreplaceable beauty of our planet. They illustrate the incredible diversity of earth's life and its landscapes. Each and every site is unique and invaluable.

Ancient places of mystery and beauty such as Kakadu in the 'top end' of Australia, Machu Picchu in Peru and the United States' Grand Canyon. The wild, windswept mountains and ice-filled valleys of New Zealand's South Island. The dark and steamy heart of Africa. The fragile splendour of Australia's Great Barrier Reef. The 'roof of the world' in Nepal and northern India. The dry and timeless plateaus of northern Africa. These are the places that make 'Paradise on Earth'.

All of these places are protected in a very special way, for all are World Heritage sites, yet all are under threat. Unfortunately, as the plundering of the world's natural resources proceeds unabated, as humans scramble for their livelihood and riches, many places of outstanding beauty and value, even those which have been set aside as places of 'outstanding universal significance', are being degraded or destroyed.

We need to heed the wisdom of our predecessors so that we can save what remains; in the words of Arkady from Bruce Chatwin's book, we need to understand that ' To wound the earth is to wound yourself, and if others wound the earth, they are wounding you '. International treaties like the World Heritage Convention are a beginning, not an end. Like the sites it protects, this convention is a fragile creation, it must be nurtured and watered so that it will grow and become more effective. We must increase awareness of what World Heritage is, so that more people will come to see the benefits of utilizing international co-operation to preserve these places.

I am proud to be part of a national government which has contributed so much to identifying and conserving Australia's World's Heritage sites, and as a member of UNESCO's Executive Board, I am proud of the magnificent and vital work this organization carries out through its World Heritage Center. I am also proud to be associated with this magnificent publication: 'Paradise on Earth' is worthy of our attention.

Hon. Barry Jones A.O. M.P.
Member of the Executive Board of UNESCO

FOREWORD

In times past, before humankind had exploited the planet beyond a certain threshold, nature could defend and replenish itself. This is no longer possible, even in the remote regions of the world. If nature is to be preserved, a new symbiosis between people and nature is needed, with an ethical dimension that places human responsibility at the center.

One effective vehicle for addressing this task is the World Heritage Convention. The object of the convention is to ensure that there are many areas of value which can be appreciated and enjoyed now and which will also be our legacy to future generations. For the natural heritage this means a conscious effort to establish a worldwide network of parks and nature reserves that encapsulate the beauty and diversity of our magnificent world. Identifying a select number of the most prominent of these for inscription on the World Heritage List has been a major role of IUCN since the first sites were inscribed in 1978. Today the World Heritage Committee has accepted over 100 natural sites as well as more than 300 cultural areas for their 'honors list'.

But defining the geography of the superlative is not enough. Experience has shown that the simple listing of a site does not guarantee protection. Each of these areas must be given special attention if it is to maintain its integrity. Sadly, the threats to World Heritage sites around the globe are growing. The convention itself, partly through its assistance fund and partly through moral pressure, has been successful on many occasions in helping to avert or, at least, mitigate many of these threats. Nonetheless, a more concerted effort will be needed in future if nature's 'hall of fame' is to remain intact.

Hence the rationale for this book. Recognition of the need for heritage conservation needs to be much expanded. More political commitment is called for. This will only come about if there is widespread public support and there will only be public support where there is a solid awareness of the benefits to society, present and future, of maintaining heritage areas. In the wise words of the African ecologist Baba Dioum:

In the end we will conserve what we love.

We will only love what we understand.

We will understand only what we learn.

Personal commitment is the key. This book celebrates the remarkable natural places that have been listed under the World Heritage Convention and the ways they meet the various criteria for selection. I urge all those who read 'Paradise on Earth' not to use it just for armchair travel. I trust that it will also spur interest and action in protecting the world's natural treasures.

Join with us. Enjoy this world of ours and, in so doing help to preserve its beauty and uniqueness for those who will come after us.

David McDowell
Director General
IUCN - The World Conservation Union

(FACING PAGE) Tasmanian devil.

(ABOVE) Square-lipped, or white rhinoceros.

INTRODUCTION

For the past decade I have had the enviable task of serving as IUCN - The World Conservation Union's scientific advisor to the UNESCO World Heritage Committee. It is enviable because it serves a noble purpose and because, after numerous site evaluations, it provides me with a global vantage point from which to view the state of conservation of the world's protected areas.

The World Heritage Convention gives equal weight to both cultural and natural heritage. In practice, however, natural sites comprise around 25% of the list. It is these sites that are the domain of both my activities with IUCN and of 'Paradise on Earth'. This superb publication catalogues each and every natural site with thoughtful commentary, displaying nature's 'hall of fame' in all of its spectacular and colorful glory.

Every year an average of a dozen new natural sites are proposed for consideration at the World Heritage Committee annual meeting. These go through a rigorous assessment process that follows five steps and only about 50% of nominations are finally inscribed, with the committee usually in accord with the advice given by the IUCN.

EVALUATION

The evaluation process is complicated by the fact that the convention does not provide definitions of the terms 'universal', 'outstanding' or 'natural'. What makes an area globally significant, as distinct to nationally significant? These terms are not easy to measure. There are, however, two approaches used to gauge the importance of a nominated site. The first is to compare it to other sites, but as Wordsworth suggested in his 1835 Guide to the Lakes District,

'...Nothing is more injurious to genuine feeling than the practice of hastily and ungraciously depreciating the face of one country by comparing it with that of another.'

Nevertheless it is possible to say for example, that the stone forests of Lunan are not as well-developed as those in Mulu in Sarawak or as the Tsingy in Madagascar. Likewise the Cocos Islands of Costa Rica were not deemed as important to science as the Galapagos in Ecuador. Nor did Viet Nam's Cuc Phuong National Park prove to be the most biodiverse reserve in Indochina. Second best was thus not good enough, and in these three cases none were approved for listing. Of course

every geographical entity, like every person, is unique, it is just that some are more unique than others!

A second means used to evaluate sites is a set of five factors which together provide an indicator of the conservation importance of the area. These are:

Distinctiveness - does the site contain species, habitats or physical features not duplicated elsewhere?

Integrity - does the site function as a reasonably self-contained unit?

Naturalness - to what extent has the site been affected by human activities?

Dependency - how critical is the site to key species and ecosystems?

Diversity - what diversity of species, habitat types and natural features does the site contain?

Obviously an area that scored high on several of the above indicators would likely be of World Heritage calibre. I would emphasize here that the end point of this exercise is to provide objective advice to the committee on the relative merits of sites in order to ensure that only the 'best' sites are accepted and the 'currency' does not become devalued .

MONITORING

Certainly being on the World Heritage List is an honor, but, unfortunately, it is no guarantee that the sanctity of an area will be safeguarded. It may come as a surprise that even many of our cherished national parks are in danger and many are losing their natural integrity with each passing year. Even World Heritage sites, the pinnacle of the world's park system and afforded the highest level of international protection are not immune from a variety of threats. The possible future removal of some sites from the prestigious World Heritage List is already being discussed. A monitoring system is thus in place which has proven very effective and in a sense IUCN is playing an 'environmental amnesty' role on behalf of the world's natural heritage.

World Heritage sites, like protected areas everywhere, are subject to a wide range of threats. There are fundamental differences between OECD and non-OECD countries in the types of threats faced: in non-OECD countries, for instance, poaching is reported to be a threat in 40% of cases, while the loss (due to human encroachment) of exotic fauna and flora is the main threat in OECD nations. The impact of tourism is one concern, however, shared by both.

Two conclusions can be drawn from any overview of the threats facing World Heritage sites: firstly, many existing sites are at high risk and we will all suffer losses if the threats are not diffused; and secondly, we cannot rest at just inscribing a site on a list - active follow-up and monitoring is needed to detect early-warning signals. Vigilance and stewardship are the keywords here.

ASSISTANCE

Unfortunately, the total amount of direct assistance from the World Heritage Fund to natural sites amounts to less than half a million dollars a year. Clearly the fund has only minimal capacity to address the challenges. It is sobering to reflect on the limited amount available to reinforce protection of the world's natural treasures. Surely this must be due to a lack of awareness of exactly what, and how much, is at stake?

PROMOTION

An important area of IUCN work on the convention is promotion. This basically involves public awareness activities, publications and advice to state parties .

'Paradise on Earth' is an important part of this work. Some of the proceeds from the sale of this magnificent encyclopedia of the superlative will go to World Heritage site protection.

POSTERITY -THE DRIVING FORCE

Several years ago I was called to Australia to examine what proved to be a successful World Heritage nomination for the sub-tropical forests of NSW. These forests had been the subject of a long and contentious battle between foresters and conservationists and in this case, the latter won. The inscription of 2,420,000ac (1, 008,000ha) of forest on the World Heritage List in 1986 was the culminating point of their protection. The State Premier then made what I felt was an exceptional statement, Premier Wran said:

'100 years from now, after we are all dead and gone, the one single act for which our government will be most remembered will be our action to protect these forests'.

The Premier was reflecting one of the eight moral laws of humankind in his statement: that is that we have a duty to posterity. This, of course, is the essential idea behind the concept of World Heritage - it implies there is something to be inherited by the generations that will follow us.

I was once asked what were the lessons from my experience in conservation. An old gravestone in Cumberland carries an inscription which perhaps best sums up my feelings:

The Wonders of the World

The Beauty and the Power

The Shape of things

Their Colours, Lights and Shades

These I saw

Look ye also while life lasts.

Dr. Jim Thorsell

Senior Advisor, Natural Heritage

IUCN - The World Conservation Union

FAUNA

- Dja has an impressive population of primates, which includes lowland gorilla, greater white-nosed guenon, moustached guenon, crowned guenon, talapoin, white-collared mangabey, white-cheeked mangabey, agile mangabey, drill, mandrill, potto, demidorff's galago, black and white colobus monkey and chimpanzee.
- Other mammals include elephant, bongo, sitatunga, buffalo, leopard, warthog, giant forest hog, and pangolin.
- Birds include Bates weaver, which is endemic to southern Cameroon, and grey-necked picathartes.
- Reptiles include python, lizard and two species of crocodile (both of which are threatened species).

FACILITIES

There are absolutely no tourist facilities in Dja Faunal Reserve, and there are no permanent scientific or research facilities. The park warden's headquarters is located at Messamena. As the Dja river is such an effective natural boundary, there are only three auxiliary guard posts, in the east and north-east of the park.

Close-up of a female crowned guenon.

be saved: for the pygmies who live there, as well as for all other peoples. Preservation must be seen as a joint international responsibility, and the West in particular should not expect nations experiencing economic difficulties to make preservation choices without some kind of economic support. The world is opening up on an unprecedented scale, and Dja cannot rely upon its inaccessibility to protect it, for the sad truth appears to be that, even protected by its river and cliffs, Dja will not remain impregnable forever.

MANOVO-GOUNDA ST FLORIS
NATIONAL PARK

MANOVO-GOUNDA-ST FLORIS NATIONAL PARK

LOCATION

Between the Manovo River and the border with Chad, Central African Republic. N 08° 05' to 09° 50', E 20° 28' to 22° 22'.

AREA

4,297,800ac (1,740,000ha).

FEATURES

- The north is made up of an extensive flood plain rich in alluvial soil and important during the hot, dry season, from December to May.
- The center is a transitional area of undulating savanna.
- The south is dominated by the sandstone Massif des Bongo, the source of the park's five main rivers.

FLORA

- The predominant vegetation type over much of the park is open woodland and savanna, intermingled with scrub or 'ironstone meadow'; on the high ground are stands of bamboo, and woods gathered around the sources of the rivers.

Located between the Manovo River and the border with Chad, and close to the border with Sudan, Manovo-Gounda-St Floris National Park was created in 1979 and is an immense park, covering 4,297,800ac (1,740,000ha), of which there are three basic zones. In the north is the extensive flood plain of the Bahr Kameur and Bahr Aouk, which, despite poor drainage, is rich in alluvial soil deposits. In the center is a transitional area of undulating savanna land that ends dramatically further south in an escarpment which announces the beginning of the sandstone Massif des Bongo. The massif is the source of the five main rivers that flow through the park to the Bahr Aouk and Bahr Kameur during the wet season, from June to November. Stands of bamboo, open savanna and woods are found on the higher ground. The predominant vegetation type over much of the park is woodland savanna, intermingled with scrub or 'ironstone meadow'. The savanna is vital to the park's grazing animals during the dry season, when they depend upon the park's perennial grasslands particularly in the flood plain in the north.

Once one of Africa's greatest wildlife reserves, with a magnificent distribution of grazing animals - and their predators - the national park has suffered recently from its proximity to two countries which have been gripped by civil war since the early 1980s: Chad and Sudan. The prolonged fighting in these two nations, largely ignored by the rest of the world, has devastated their economies, caused massive refugee movement, and seen an enormous influx of firearms into the region. This last problem has proved particularly disastrous for Manovo-Gounda-St Floris, with bandits entering the national park with automatic weapons. Poachers not only outnumbered park wardens, but also possessed infinitely superior firepower.

Most of the poachers are from outside The Central African Republic, and are suspected of being actual combatants in the wars in Sudan and Chad, who have turned to poaching as the easiest means of obtaining hard currency. Thanks to the

incessant demand for items like rhino horn in Taiwan, Hong Kong and China, not only has the national park's black rhinoceros population been all but annihilated, but weapons purchased with cash raised from the sale of the horn are later often turned upon civilians. Perhaps nowhere is the interconnection between the welfare of animals and humans as evident as in this situation where animals are killed for profit so that weapons may be purchased to continue apparently unending warfare.

Grave concern has recently been expressed at plans to transfer management of this park to a private foundation. It can only be hoped that good sense will prevail and these plans will be dropped.

Rarely have recent statistics looked as bleak as those in Manovo-Gounda-St Floris: between 1981 and 1984, the national park's elephant population was reduced by 75%; there are now only about ten black rhinos left in all of the park; giraffe numbers continue to fall. Still, in the face of such gloom, and desperately underfinanced and understaffed, the park wardens persevere, trying to save what is left, which after all does include a vast array of animals including cheetah, lion, leopard, giant eland, hunting dog, warthog, and hippopotamus. Shoebill crocodile, like the park's leopard population, once also subjected to poaching, is still found. Among the primates are barber baboon, tantalus monkey, colobus monkey, and greater white-nosed monkey.

Luckily the park's impressive bird colonies, which include more than 320 species, are still flourishing, particularly aquatic birds in the northern flood plains. Pelican and stork are common, and there are over 20 species of birds of prey, including African fish eagle. Ostrich is found on the plains, while along the rivers are bee-eaters and kingfishers.

There is also an extensive number of ungulates, or hoofed animals, such as the kob; duiker; waterbuck; hartebeest; topi; roan antelope; and reedbuck. These grazing animals are still competing with illegal domestic herds brought into the park in the dry season by nomads from Chad and the Nyala region of Sudan. There are worries this will have a long-term detrimental effect on the composition of the park's grasslands, and campfires started by illegal herdsmen are a constant menace in the fierce heat of the dry season.

Topi - found, along with several other species of ungulate, in vast numbers.

- The perennial grasslands, particularly in the north, are of enormous importance during the dry season for the park's vast herds of grazing animals.

FAUNA

- The park's herds of black rhinoceros and elephant have been devastated by poaching in the last decade or two.
- Giraffe, leopard and shoebill crocodile have also been affected by poaching.
- Primates include barber baboon, and tantalus, colobus, and greater white-nosed monkeys.
- There are over 320 species of birds, including African fish eagle, ostrich, and several species of bee-eater and kingfisher.
- Ungulates such as the red-fronted gazelle, duiker, waterbuck, hartebeest, topi, and roan antelope are found in impressive numbers.

FACILITIES

Access to the park is fairly easy from the south. The northern and eastern sections should be visited with some care: poachers have been known to kill witnesses. Travel in the north is difficult during the inundations. Accommodation is very limited, although there are plans to develop the park in the future.

Manovo-Gounda
National Park—
a herd of this park's
most abundant large
mammal, the kob.

Trees and Global Warming

There is ample evidence that the destruction of forests contributes to the build up of carbon dioxide released into the atmosphere - although to a lesser extent than the burning of fossil fuels.

If the greenhouse effect has been exacerbated by the destruction of forests, can the planting of new trees and letting them grow, along with preservation of remaining natural forests, alleviate the situation?

It seems that even extensive planting of forests can only slow down the change in global climate to a relatively small extent, and only temporarily, but every little bit helps and reforestation is now being taken seriously. Moreover, planting trees does no harm, and provides many benefits. In particular, reforestation in the form of agro-forestry not only slows soil erosion and protects water tables, but, in addition, supplies indigenous people with products which they can utilize for their own needs and also market: building poles, charcoal, firewood.

It is encouraging to find that villagers in some parts of Africa are beginning to understand the dangers of soil erosion and lack of water caused by indiscriminate slash and burn agriculture. Many small tree planting programs are springing up throughout Tanzania, for example. These should be encouraged.

There are many ways in which the developed world, in an effort to slow down global warming, can assist economically poor countries to preserve their forests: debt swap for nature; developing forest tourism; carefully planning rural development programs in surrounding villages. Agro-forestry is particularly important in this respect.

Timber companies should practise selective logging whenever possible, and industrial operations, such as oil exploration, should not only be conducted in such a way as to minimize environmental damage, but in conjunction with programs designed to conserve the area as a whole.

Conserving the last of the great natural forests along with the planting and growing of trees, even though it only temporarily slows down the greenhouse effect, is, I believe, crucial. Even if we are ultimately doomed, we should strive to maintain tolerable living conditions for as long as possible for the sake of the next generation. Guarding and nurturing trees will help. It will improve the quality of life for thousands of people and their livestock, protect countless wild animals, and - at least for a while - save hundreds of animal and plant species from extinction.

DR JANE GOODALL
The Jane Goodall Institute (UK).

Rwenzori Mountains National Park, Uganda—a recent nomination for inclusion on the World Heritage List.

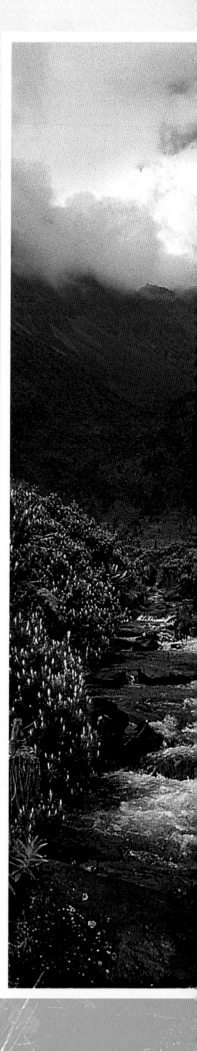

SIMEN
NATIONAL PARK

SIMEN MOUNTAIN NATIONAL PARK

LOCATION

In the western Simen Mountains, 75mi (120km) north-east of Gondar in Begemder Province, N 13° 11', E 38° 04'.

AREA

52,800ac (22,000ha).

FEATURES

The area is part of the Simen Massif which includes the highest peak in Ethiopia, Ras Dashan; the massif was formed some 25 million years ago and the igneous basalts have since been eroded to form precipitous cliffs and deep gorges.

FLORA

This is a mixture of Afro-Alpine woods, heath forest, high montane vegetation, montane savanna and montane moorland with tree heath, giant lobelia, yellow primrose, everlastings, lady's mantle and mosses.

Sitting in remote majesty atop a vast expanse of plateau grasslands, Simen National Park is a fascinating focus for observing both the splendor of nature and the grandeur of ancient civilizations. Lying not far from the archeological ruins of Aksum, where over 100 hand-carved stone monoliths, or stelae, can be found, and close to Gondar, where curious fifteenth century churches and palaces still stand, Simen National Park occupies the northern section of the Ethiopian Amhara plateau, and is part of the Simen Massif. Formed in the Miocene Epoch, erosion has cut vertiginous gorges and spectacular cliffs out of the massif. Some of these escarpments are as high as 5,000ft (1,500m), including a sequence in the north of the park 22mi (35km) in length. These sheer precipices invest Simen with an air of dramatic isolation which is enhanced by the course of the Tacazze River and its tributaries, the moat-like valleys of which bound the massif both to the south and north-east.

With its abundance of creviced basalt rock, Simen serves as an ideal water catchment area, replenished by two wet seasons and the Mayshasha River, which weaves its way north to south through the national park. Consequently, the park is rich in a wide range of wildlife and vegetation. In this mountainous environment, with altitudes ranging up to 14,600ft (4,430m), can be found alpine moss and high altitude forest as well as mountain savanna and moorlands. The region's two most important mammals are endangered: the walia ibex, a species of wild mountain goat endemic to the massif itself, and the Simen fox, which is only found in parts of Ethiopia. The walia ibex's existence has been threatened by the cross-breeding of this species with the domestic goat. A captive breeding program will soon be introduced to halt the complete hybridization of this species. The Simen fox is menaced by loss of habitat, poaching, and by competition for prey. It is just one of several carnivores which have been experiencing a decline in the last few decades. Others include the leopard, the serval, and the wild cat.

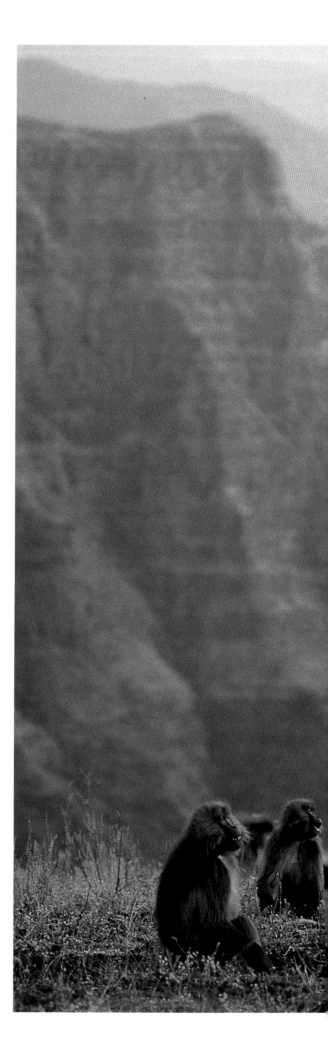

FAUNA

- A total of 21 mammals have been recorded, with three endemics and 63 bird species, including seven endemics.
- Walia ibex is endemic to Simen Mountain, Simen Fox is endemic to Ethiopia.
- Other mammals include gelada baboon, hamadryas baboon, colobus monkey, serval, leopard, caracal, wild cat, spotted hyena, jackal, and several large herbivores including bushbuck, common duiker, and klipspringer.
- The 400 bird species include lammergeier, Verreaux's eagle, kestrel, lanner falcon and augur buzzard.

FACILITIES

The basic tourist facilities which had catered to a handful of visitors every year fell into a state of disrepair during the war, when the whole area was off limits. While the region has since opened up, access into and around the park remains difficult. The country's new authorities have made tourism, scientific research and education the future major priorities for the park.

A group of gelada baboons make a peaceful scene set against the dramatic backdrop of Simen massif.

Two carrion-eaters, the jackal and the spotted hyena, have long been the subject of prejudices, and the latter is especially despized and feared.

Prejudice and superstitions however pose less of a threat to Simen's wildlife than the loss of habitat which is caused by grass burning and defor-estation. Forests of St-John's-wort, which once flourished at altitudes up to 13,200ft (4,000m), have now all but disappeared. As the highlands of Ethiopia have always been one of the most heavily populated farming regions on the continent, Simen has always been particularly vulnerable to damage caused by overgrazing and clearing for fuel.

Simen itself has been the site of cultivation for at least 2,000 years. When it was made a national park, the region supported about 2,500 farmers, practising traditional methods of agriculture, and competing with the carnivores for game such as bushpig and bushbuck. In 1979, much of the local farming community was forcibly removed. Around 700 farmers remain, today using about a third of the park for agriculture and grazing. The question of how to reconcile rescuing a fragile natural site together with its exceptional species of flora and fauna without disrupting or even endangering the livelihood of its human inhabitants who exercise convincing traditional and cultural claims to the land, is one of the most agonizing to be faced in the modern world. Perhaps nowhere is this choice more potent than in Ethiopia, which has suffered as few nations have over the last two decades. If there is any absolute truth in the struggle to conserve what is left of our earth's diminishing natural environment, it is that there are never any easy solutions.

The famine and civil war which brought unparalleled suffering to Ethiopia left their marks on Simen as well, and for a time the national park was occupied by the Tigre People's Liberation Army. Now that the war is over, World Heritage funds are being used to rehabilitate the park.

A Simen fox digs for food - probably a small rodent.

(FAR LEFT) Part of the Tacazze river system in Simen.

MOUNT NIMBA
RESERVES

MOUNT NIMBA RESERVES

LOCATION

The massif of Nimba is situated on the border between Guinea, The Ivory Coast, and Liberia, some 12mi (20km) from the town of Lola and 39mi (62km) from N'Zérékoré, N 07° 18', W 10° 35'.

AREA

The Guinean Nature Reserve is 41,100ac (17,130ha), while the Ivory Coast Nature Reserve is 11 000ac (5,000ha).

FEATURES

The Nimba massif, also known as the 'Guinean backbone', rises up from the relatively level surrounding countryside to a maximum height of 5,780ft (1,752m), forming an immense wall that travels along a south-west to north-east axis. Its striking, silhouetted summits of high altitude grassland and wooded slopes contrasts sharply with its sheer cliffs and ridges.

FLORA

- There are three major vegetation types: (i) high altitude grassland; (ii) plains savanna; (iii) predominantly primary forest.
- More than 2,000 plant species have been described from the area, and about 16 are thought to be endemic.

The 'Guinean backbone'.

One of the growing number of World Heritage sites shared between two nations, the Nimba Massif runs along the borders of the three West African nations of Guinea, the Ivory Coast and Liberia, with the Liberian portion of the massif excluded from the World Heritage site.

The Nimba massif, also known as the 'Guinean backbone', rises up from the relatively level surrounding countryside to a maximum height of 5,780ft (1,752m), forming an immense wall that travels along a south-west to north-east axis. Its striking, silhouetted summits of high altitude grassland and wooded slopes contrast sharply with its sheer cliffs and ridges. It is a product of massive erosion; as surrounding rock was slowly weathered away, it left behind a hard core of ore-bearing quartzite: what we now know as the massif.

Around it, at an altitude of 1,650ft (500m), is an expanse of savanna grasslands. In all, the Guinean Nature Reserve is 41,100ac (17,130ha), while the Ivory Coast Nature Reserve is 11,000ac (5,000ha). A plan to join these reserves to a proposed Liberian reserve, to be created out of an area badly degraded by ore-mining, has been shattered by the Liberian Civil War.

As well as possessing a stark beauty enhanced by a sense of dramatic isolation, the Nimba Mountains are vital to the region's water supply. They are the source of both the Cavally and the Ya Rivers, as well as many smaller streams. Its valleys are deep and covered mainly in primary rainforest, which extends up to the foothills. There is an enormous topographical diversity to the two nature reserves, with plateaux, plains savanna, rounded hills and jagged peaks all to be found.

There are over 200 endemic species among the reserves' 500 species of fauna: a rich diversification reflecting the presence of grasslands and forests. Among the most unusual animals are two species of toad which are viviparous - they bring forth their young live and not as eggs, as with almost all other amphibians. Also found are chimpanzees; the lesser bushbaby; the palm civet and its cousin, the genet; lions; various species of duiker, the small, short-horned antelope; leopards; and pygmy hippopotamuses.

- There are over 200 endemic species among the reserves' 500 species of fauna.
- Mammals include chimpanzees; the lesser bushbaby; the palm civet and its cousin, the genet; lions; various species of duiker, the small, short-horned antelope; leopards; and pygmy hippopotamuses.

FACILITIES

There are no tourist facilities as tourism is forbidden inside both reserves. At the moment there are six patrol stations within the reserves, and a research station of the French Institute for Black Africa, IFAN, is located in the northern section of the massif.

A clawless otter enjoys its fresh kill.

While there are no settlements on the mountains themselves, there are ten villages in the immediate vicinity, home to several thousand crop farmers who unfortunately often practice large-scale slash and burn agriculture. This is but one of several threats to an area which, because of its aspect of secluded splendor, would seem to be beyond the usual hazards to nature. Sadly this is far from the case.

The greatest challenge to the integrity of the Mount Nimba Reserves comes in the form of extensive iron-ore mining. Mining in the Liberian section of the Nimba Massif, as well as in a northern section within Guinea which is not a part of the World Heritage site, has led to sizeable areas of soil being removed from the land. This has resulted in the poisoning of streams from heavy metal run-off. After the ore deposits in Liberia are exhausted, there are plans to shift the search for ore to the central Guinean section of Mount Nimba. It is believed that 300 million tonnes of iron ore will be extracted over 25 years. This immense operation will directly effect some 480ac (200ha), but of course a larger area of about 2,400ac (1,000ha) will be affected via heavy metal run-offs into streams and the inevitable collateral

damage caused simply by lodging workers, transporting mined ore and disrupting the habitat of what is still essentially an uninhabited mountain chain.

Another menace to Mount Nimba comes from the extremely bloody civil war in Liberia, which has been raging for several years, creating great devastation, causing refugees to flee into neighboring countries in vast numbers, inevitably disrupting local populations and food supplies, and creating an element of instability. Ironically, it is this very war which is holding up plans to begin mining in Guinean Mount Nimba, as the Liberian railway line from Mount Nimba to the deep-water port of Buchanan in Liberia is essential for the commercial viability of the mining operation.

As the Mount Nimba Reserves have attracted intense scientific interest, particularly the study of primates, high altitude grasslands, and the collection of meteorological data, it has been suggested that a permanent tropical ecology station ought to be established. It remains to be seen whether such a project will engender the kind of support that iron-ore mining obviously enjoys.

COMOE
NATIONAL PARK

COMOE NATIONAL PARK

LOCATION

Extending from 22mi (35km) south-west of Bouna, in the north-east préfectures of Bouna and Ferkessedougou, westwards across the Comoe River to the vicinity of Kong. 375mi (600km) from Abidjan, N 08° 05' to 09° 06', W 03° 01' to 04° 04'.

AREA

2,760,000ac (1,150,000ha).

FLORA

• The majority of the park (approximately 90%) is open forest and savanna woodland.

• There are large areas of riparian grassland scattered throughout the park and the landscape of the grassy plains is varied by thickets, there are also smaller amounts of gallery forest as well as dense dry forest.

Comoe National Park exhibits a fascinating transition from forest to savanna, and includes many other specialized ecosystems. It covers 2,760,000ac (1,150,000ha) of the area between the Comoe and the Volta rivers where there is an inter-fluvial plain of schist and granite. A series of ridges and granite 'inselbergs' rises a further 1,000ft (300m) above the plain to an altitude of approximately 2,000ft (600m). The soil is unsuitable for cultivation although there is an abundance of permanent as well as semi-permanent water and a rich variety of native flora.

The climate is also transitional with a Sudan type humidity which is almost tropical, and a single dry season of six months in the north and eight months in the south. Vegetation is more prevalent in the south, possibly benefiting from the long period of dryness. The majority of the park (approximately 90%) is open forest and savanna woodland. Most of the forest trees are leguminous. There are large areas of riparian grassland scattered throughout the park and the landscape of the grassy plains is varied by thickets of *Bauhinia*, *Combretum* and *Gardenia*. There are also smaller amounts of gallery forest as well as dense dry forest. The floodplains and the rocky inselbergs have their own peculiar habitats.

The park is the most northerly place on the African continent where yellow backed duiker and bongo can be found. Eleven species of monkey inhabit the park's forests including Diana monkey, green monkey, mona monkey, lesser white-nosed monkey, white collared mangabey, chimpanzee, anubis baboon and black and white colobus. There are also many species of carnivore including lion, leopard, rock hyrax and aardvark. Other animals found in the park are elephant, hippopotamus, bushbuck, bushpig, warthog, sitatunga, buffalo, roan antelope, kob and oribi. The wetlands attract an enormous number and range of birds. There are many predatory birds including five, out of a total of six, west African species of vulture. Smaller birds include ducks, plovers and francolins. Grey and Goliath heron are just two of the ten heron species

to be found along with other large waterbirds - the yellow-billed egret, black-winged stilt and four west African stork species. Also found in the waterways of the park are all three species of African crocodile, the slender-snouted, Nile and dwarf.

The presence of an insect, the black fly, has effectively protected the park from human interference. This fly is the source of a particularly nasty affliction known as 'river blindness', and its presence has discouraged substantial human encroachment. However uncontrolled burning and

(ABOVE)
Dwarf crocodiles.

cattle grazing in the south are still problems. Poaching has decreased since the introduction of an anti-poaching campaign in 1974. But the park, protected naturally and now legally from human interference, now faces the heavy strain of a growing tourist industry. Tourism is a necessary source of funds needed to maintain the park but, as is the case now in many underdeveloped countries around the globe, it is a difficult matter to balance the benefits of the 'tourist dollar' against the further maintenance costs which tourism incurs. It is also difficult to know just where to draw the fine line which balances the obvious financial benefits of tourism with the damage which it will inevitably cause. Somewhat fortunately, tourists are further restricted by a natural barrier, as the park is inaccessible in the wet season and therefore only open to tourists between November and April.

TAI
NATIONAL PARK

TAI
NATIONAL PARK

LOCATION

In the south-west of The Ivory Coast, about 132mi (200km) south of Man and 66mi (100km) from the coast, in the districts of Guiglo and Sassandra, N 05° 15' to 06° 07', W 07° 25' to 07° 54'.

AREA

792,000ac (330,000ha).

FEATURES

The importance of this national park lies in the fact that it's the final remnant of a massive stretch of virgin forest which once encompassed most of the southern region of West Africa, an area which today includes The Ivory Coast, Liberia, Ghana and Sierra Leone.

FLORA

- Over 1,300 species of higher plants are found in the park.
- 16% of all flora species catalogued in Tai National Park (representing more than 150 species) are endemic.
- The top strata of the forest is dominated by giant trees which can attain heights of up to 200ft (60m), they are evergreens with very thick trunks, often buttressed with dense root systems.
- Smaller trees, ferns, mosses and lichens flourish on the dark, damp forest floor.

(ABOVE) A view of Tai's remarkable forest canopy.

This 792,000ac (330,000ha) national park is the final remnant of a massive stretch of virgin forest which once encompassed most of the southern region of West Africa, an area which today includes The Ivory Coast, Liberia, Ghana and Sierra Leone. It is vitally important to preserve this island of forest - which ranges from palms and ebony to swamp forest and which includes over 1,300 species of higher plant - given the frightening rapidity with which the rest of this once enormous stretch of forest has disappeared.

We can get an idea of the loss represented by this destruction of habitat when we examine what has been found in this remaining stretch of forest - a staggering 16% of all flora species catalogued in Tai National Park (representing more than 150 species) are endemic: plants long thought extinct have been found in this park.

Tai offers a wonderful example of the various 'stratas' that are to be found in dense primary forest. The top strata, or layer, is dominated by the giants - trees which attain heights of up to 198ft (60m). Here, these giants tend to be evergreens with very thick trunks, often heavily buttressed, with dense root systems. They spread their huge branches out into an interlocking network, forming a canopy that ensures that the earth below exists in a state of perpetual near-obscurity. In the dank, moist darkness closer to the earth, pungent with decaying organic matter, smaller trees, ferns, mosses and lichens flourish.

These forests make an ideal home for the park's colonies of chimpanzees. The population of these social, active primates is estimated to be somewhere between 2,000 and 2,800. In the past chimpanzees were often needlessly killed, just so hunters could steal baby chimpanzees, which would then be sold to zoos, or bred for scientific research. Tai also has an exceptionally rich monkey population with many species present including

mona, white-nosed and Diana monkeys. There are also three types of pangolin, or scaled-anteater, and a great variety of duiker antelopes.

As elsewhere in Africa, the elephant population of Tai has seen a tragic, perhaps irreversible, decline in numbers over a relatively short period of time. There were nearly 2,000 at the end of the 1970's; today there are probably less than 100. Tai appeared to be losing the war against poachers, who butchered the elephants for their tusks, but the impact of the ivory moratorium has apparently slowed things down enough to perhaps preserve Tai's remaining elephants. Other animals slaughtered by poachers include leopards for their pelts, crocodiles for their skin, and monkeys for food.

Intruders searching for gold have posed a serious threat to the integrity of Tai in recent times. These prospectors do a surprising amount of damage, following river systems where they clear forest in low-lying zones to make room for their digs. As has so often been the case in South America, they act as a kind of vanguard for the slash and burn agriculturalists who almost inevitably follow them.

The greatest threat of all comes from organized loggers, who seek Tai's precious timber, including such prized wood as ebony. After independence, Tai provided The Ivory Coast with most of its timber. Despite the government since having withdrawn all timber concessions, the logging continues. A buffer zone of 48,000ac (20,000ha), consisting of a three mile boundary which virtually surrounds the park and which was designed to protect it, has itself been heavily logged, and deep incursions have been made from it into the park proper in the east; while the north remains susceptible to intrusions by logging and agricultural interests. A road which was designed to accentuate the boundaries of the national park has merely provided easier access to it for loggers, miners, illegal farmers and poachers.

The south-west portion of Tai has always been denser in growth, because of higher rainfall, richer soil and its very inaccessibility. But with the construction of the perimeter road, this region is now also under threat. The pattern is depressingly familiar. After areas are cleared-felled, a particularly wasteful way of logging, agriculturalists move in and install commodity crops such as cocoa and coffee, even though the value of these has slumped to an all-time low. Thus something unique and beautiful is systematically being replaced by 'cash crops' which have been subjected to a world-wide glut for the past decade. Subsistence crops such as yams, okra and sweet potato are also planted. To deal with all these problems, the government hopes to have the legal status of the park affirmed in local courts, which would allow the expulsion of gold miners once and for all. It has also proposed destroying all farms within the park, and enlarging the park with the addition of neighboring primary forest in the south and by perhaps reincorporating the N'Zo Fauna Reserve, which was taken out of the park in 1972, back into Tai National Park.

TSINGY DE BEMARAHA
STRICT NATURE RESERVE

LOCATION

In the northern sector of the Antsingy region of the Bemaraha Plateau, north of the Manambolo River Gorge, S 18° 17' to 19° 06', E 44° 36' to 44° 58'.

AREA

375,440ac (152,000ha).

FEATURES

- The Bemaraha Plateau is a rugged massif with limestone karst features, rounded sloping hillocks in the west, and sheer cliffs up to 1,312ft (400m) in the east. The southern region is famous for its 'limestone forest'.
- There are scattered remains of ancient cemeteries which allegedly contain the remnants of the island's first inhabitants, the 'Vazimbas'.
- The plateau's perennial and seasonal rivers are vital to the western part of the island, which relies upon the Tsingy de Bemaraha for its water, particularly during the dry season, which lasts from April to November.

FLORA

- The vegetation consists of dense, dry forest and savanna grasslands.

The elusive aye-aye (ABOVE) and a brown lemur (BELOW).

The nature reserve lies inland from the west coast of the island of Madagascar, occupying a part of the Bemaraha Plateau, a rugged massif with limestone karst features, rounded sloping hillocks in the west, and, in the east, sheer cliffs up to 1,312ft (400m) high which plunge spectacularly down to the Manambolo River, forming a long, impenetrable wall which runs for miles in a north-south direction. This is a remote, sometimes harsh landscape, its isolated, strange beauty particularly strong in the southern region, its famous pinnacles and outcrops fashioning an extraordinary vista of jagged pillars, columns, towers and eruptions which have been compared to a 'limestone forest'. This fascinating, and occasionally foreboding, reserve is home to some of the most unique and threatened wildlife and flora to be found anywhere, including the intensely shy Lemur. There are also scattered remains of ancient cemeteries which, according to local tradition, contain the remnants of Madagascar's first inhabitants, the mysterious 'Vazimbas' people.

- Ebony, wild banana, and baobab are common.
- Xerophytic plants grow near rocky outcrops, the best known of these being the aloe.

FAUNA

- Tsingy de Bemaraha is the only site in the world where the Brookesia perarmata chameleon is found.
- Several different types of lemur, an intensely shy arboreal primate, are found here and there are unconfirmed sightings of the nocturnal aye-aye.
- Over 50 species of bird have been sighted here, including goshawk, Madagascan owl, and Madagascan grey-throated rail.

FACILITIES

Entry into the Tsingy de Bemaraha Strict Nature Reserve is forbidden to all except those engaged in scientific study, and visits are usually restricted to either the northern forests or the southern limestone pinnacles. These overnight trips are organized by guides based at the forest station at Antsalova, where the chief of the reserve lives, and at Bekopaka, where there is a small guard outpost. While options for opening up the region to tourism are currently being studied, there are no facilities inside the reserve at all, and the nearest accommodation is in Maintirano, 93mi (150km) away.

(LEFT) Mouse lemur.

Golden bamboo lemur.

Both perennial and seasonal rivers course through the plateau, the latter appearing during the wet season when almost 40in (1,000mm) of rain falls. This sequence of rivers is hugely important for western Madagascar, which has a low rainfall and is heavily dependent upon the Tsingy de Bemaraha for its water, particularly during the dry season, which lasts from April to November.

The vegetation consists of either dense, very dry forest which is typical of western Madagascar's limestone plateaux, or savanna grasslands. Ebony, wild banana, and baobab are present, and near rocky outcrops can be found a number of xerophytic plants the best known being Aloe, often used in the pharmaceutical and cosmetics industries.

The wildlife of Tsingy de Bemaraha has not been subject to much scientific study on account of a lack of funds, but it is known to harbor a number of rare animals, and is the only site where the species of chameleon Brookesia perarmata is found, as well as several different types of lemur. Although lemurs are notoriously difficult to see, living almost all of their lives in trees, where they leap from one branch to another with an eerie, silent effortlessness, they are renowned for their high-pitched cry which penetrates dense forest, and which is usually heard around sunset or dawn. There have also been as yet unconfirmed sightings of aye-aye, a nocturnal lemur, its onomatopoeic name reflecting its cry. Some 50 species of bird have been recorded here including goshawk; Madagascan owl; and Madagascan grey-throated rail.

Because of its inaccessible landscape, the southern region with its 'limestone forest' pinnacles has been spared the intrusions by herders experienced in other parts of the reserve. These herders often burn off sections of forest to provide access to grasslands for their cattle, a dangerous as well as destructive act given the dryness of parts of the plateau. Yet little can be done to curb such illegal incursions, as there is not enough money to even mark the boundaries of the nature reserve, let alone patrol it. It is thought that many of the local inhabitants aren't even aware of its existence.

A pair of boabab trees.

(LEFT) A rare glimpse of a mother lemur and her baby.

(ABOVE) The rugged
and spectacular
'limestone forest'.

Two more of this reserves
remarkable lemur
population: the verreaux
cifaka (RIGHT) and the
indri (FAR RIGHT).

LAKE MALAWI
NATIONAL PARK

**LAKE MALAWI
NATIONAL PARK**

LOCATION

On the Nankumba
Peninsula at the
southern end of Lake
Malawi, in Mangochi
District, Southern Region
of Malawi, approxi-
mately,
S 14° 02', E 34° 53'.

AREA

23,200ac (9,400ha).

FEATURES

- The lake is famous for
  its delicately balanced
  water, and requires
  1,700 years to
  completely renew
  itself.
- The waters contain
  more fish species than
  any other lake in the
  world.
- The lake is part of the
  great Rift Valley,
  where human life
  began.

FLORA

- There are rich weed
  and reed beds at the
  bottom of the lake.
- The surrounding hills,
  once heavily wooded
  with baobab, have
  been seriously
  logged, and unsightly
  scrub has moved in
  on many areas.

FAUNA

- There are 500 fish
  species in the lake,
  90% of which are
  endemic. Most of the
  endemic species are
  from the cichlidae, a
  kind of spiny fish.
  Lake Malawi accounts
  for 30% of all
  cichlidae species on
  earth.

(ABOVE)
*Mbuna - young cichlid
enter their mother's
mouth.*

This national park is located across the southern stretch of Lake Malawi, a huge lake which occupies a fifth of the entire country. The lake is exceptional for several reasons. It is the fourth deepest and eleventh largest lake in the world, and is famed for the purity of its waters and their astonishing transparency. Because of its tropical setting, it possesses a stratified water layer, with a thermo- cline dividing the upper warmer water from the lower cooler water. It also contains more fish species than any other lake in the world, with over 500 species from ten families, 90% of which are endemic and half of which are found in that section of the lake which is within the national park: a mere 0.04% of the lake's total area. Of the endemic species, the overwhelming majority belong to the

- Mammals include hippopotamus, leopard, greater kudu, bushbuck, zebra, impala, grey duiker, bush pig and a small population of African elephant.
- Birdlife includes fish eagle and white-breasted cormorant.
- Crocodile, and water monitor lizard flourish in the conditions.

FACILITIES

Although there are facilities such as a resthouse and camping ground at Cape Maclear, the site has become spoilt by unauthorized shacks and sheds, as well as mooring for power boats which are a significant source of pollution. There are plans to rebuild the area, to develop new hotels and hostels, and to organize glass-bottom boat trips. The Department of Fisheries research headquarters are at Monkey Bay.

Another member of Lake Malawi's remarkable fish population - the Pseudotropheus Aurora will always find its way home, even if released 1.5m (2km) away.

cichlidae, a kind of spiny fish also found in fresh-water bodies in Africa, South America and some parts of Southern Asia. Lake Malawi accounts for a staggering 30% of all cichlidae species on earth. The lake's most famous fish is the colorful 'mbuna' or rock-dwelling fish. The lake's underwater habitat includes both rocky and sandy zones, and there are rich weed and reed beds.

Although some of the lake's islands have enjoyed protection for the last 60 years, and much of the territory used to be forest reserve, logging in the region, particularly on the high ground overlooking the lake, has had an adverse affect on Lake Malawi's water levels, allowing too much rainwater to flow down the newly denuded hills into the lake, and upsetting the delicate balance of a body which requires 1,700 years to completely renew its waters.

Large mammals attracted to its waters include hippopotamus, leopard, greater kudu, bushbuck, zebra, impala, grey duiker, bush pig and a small population of African elephant which journey down to the lake between the Mwemya and Nkhudzi hills. Amongst the park's birds are fish eagle, which inhabit the shoreline. The islands, especially Mumbo and Boadzulu, are important

nesting areas for large colonies of white-breasted cormorant. Reptiles include crocodile, and water monitor lizard on Boadzulu island.

Lake Malawi National Park also includes the Cape Maclear Peninsula, a major headland that divides the southern part of the lake into two branches, one going to the east, the other going to the south. Apart from a few sandy inlets, particularly at Chembe-Otter Point, and some swamp, the lakeshore rapidly gives way to steeply rising hills, made mainly of biotite-granite, which can sometimes foster the illusion that the lake is a huge watery crater lying inside a vast volcano. Certainly the hills darken the lake's waters with their shadows, adding further mystery to an extraordinary site, for the lake is of ancient origins, between one to two million years old, and is part of the great Rift Valley, where it is thought human life began.

Although the surrounding hills were once heavily wooded, mainly with baobab, logging has badly scarred the landscape, especially at an altitude around 3,280ft (1,000m). Unsightly scrub has taken over areas once dense with trees. The locals cut down the timber for firewood and for carving traditional fishing poles. There are plans to create a special wooded area of 2,964ac (1,200ha) in the south of the park to provide future timber for poles and firewood. It's part of a plan to preserve what's left of the hill forests. A forestry nursery has been opened in the park, with the goal of planting 30,000 seedlings per year to reforest the peninsula and provide future fuel needs. Some limited traditional fishing is practised by the five lakeside villages inside the park. The whole lake provides an annual catch of 44,000 tons (40,000 tonnes) of fish to feed an estimated 16,000 lakeside dwellers. Fishing is prohibited 338ft (100m) from the park's shore. This protects the 'mbuna', which tends to stay close to shore, while not interfering with the livelihood of the fishermen as the fish they catch for food are generally found in the open water. The survival of the lake's unique life and its pristine waters depends largely upon the people who live by its shores.

BANC D'ARGUIN
NATIONAL PARK

Mother white pelican and her baby.

L ying between the vast expanse of the Sahara, and the even greater mass of the Atlantic, inaccessible to all but a few; the desolate, stark beauty of the Banc d'Arguin National Park is a stunning representation of a transition zone between sea and sand, and, each winter is home to the largest concentration of migratory wading birds in the world.

This low-lying park of 2,800,000ac (1,200,000ha) is equally divided between marine and terrestrial reserves, and includes fifteen main islands of varying size. The land is mainly a flat, wind-swept, sandy expanse with some scrub and sand dunes as well as mud flats, tidal flats around the largest island Tidra, and some mangrove to the north of Tidra. The maritime region roughly extends from Cap Blanc in the north to Cap

Timiris in the south. The waters between these two capes, a distance of about 100mi (160km), is remarkably shallow, reaching depths of just 16.5ft (5m) at low tide at its most westerly boundaries, nearly 36mi (60km) from shore. The calmness and the clarity of the waters is caused by an abundance of eel grass seabeds and algae fields, which soften the currents and provide a multitude of food, making Banc d'Arguin an ideal winter home to over two million water fowl: 30% of all wading birds using the Atlantic flyway. These numbers are in part due to the fact that Banc D'Arguin is located at the migratory limit of both the Palearctic (from the Northern Hemisphere) birds and the Afrotropical birds.

BANC D'ARGUIN NATIONAL PARK

LOCATION

On the Atlantic desert-coast of Mauritania, N 19° 21' to 21° 51', W 16° 00' to 16° 45'.

AREA

2,880,000ac (1,200,000ha).

FEATURES

- The 7,440ac (3,100ha) mangrove swamp in the park is a relict of a previous humid geological period when Banc d'Arguin was a vast estuary mouth for rivers flowing from the Sahara.

FLORA

- The terrestrial component of the park is represented by a Saharan vegetation with a limited Mediterranean influence. Tree species include acacias.
- In total there are some 3,360ac (1,400ha) of mangrove swamps and a further 4,080ac (1,700ha) in bays on the mainland.
- These are the most northerly stands of mangrove on the eastern shore of the Atlantic and represent relicts from the period when the coastal oueds carried fresh water from the Sahara.
- Shallow water vegetation comprises extensive seagrass beds and various seaweeds, covering a total area of 300sqmi (800sqkm).

- Winter home to over two million water fowl: 30% of all wading birds using the Atlantic flyway.
- Three million land birds also seek shelter here each winter.
- The waters attract many sea mammals, such as orcas; porpoises; and five different varieties of dolphin, including the bottle-nosed dolphin.
- The most famous of all the park's resident marine animals is the monk seal: its colony of 100 to 150 individuals is the largest known concentration of this species - unusual in being the only one which can live in tropical conditions.

FACILITIES

Access to the park is possible along the road which links the capital, Nouakchott, to the coastal community of Nouadhibou, just to the north of the park, towards the tip of Cap Blanc. Accommodation can be found in both towns. Because of the special nature of the park, tourism is strictly controlled. Inside Banc d'Arguin there are no tourist facilities as such, although there is a field station in the heart of the reserve, at Cap Iouik. Fishing, hunting, camping and low level flying are all prohibited, and pleasure craft, as a rule, cannot enter the park's marine zone.

Even more impressive than the sheer numbers of birds is their diversity, with more than 100 species being recorded. This in itself would make Banc d'Arguin of vital ornithological importance, but when one takes into account the additional three million land birds that also seek shelter here each winter, the truly exceptional qualities of the park come into focus. It is quite literally a bird paradise, and the sight of so many birds, particularly when viewed from the sea, is awe-inspiring. It is often difficult to tell where the shore ends and the sea begins, there are so many waders on the water's edge, forming large, living islands of color and sound.

Banc d'Arguin is an important breeding ground for many types of valuable commercial fish, including seabass and seabream, and is close to the migratory passage of fish such as red mullet and tuna. Unfortunately, this has encouraged foreign fishing fleets to over-fish the waters just outside the park. It is the mechanized equivalent of a feeding frenzy, with foreign fishing boats targeting an area and exploiting it until it's exhausted before moving on: a maritime version of slash and burn farming. Nations such as Mauritania, which have carefully nurtured their fishing grounds, can see all their care destroyed in a frighteningly short period of time. Usually the culprits are from the EEC or Japan: nations which have zealously overworked their own waters and are driven further and further afield, inflicting the same kind of damage to other people's fish stocks as they have inflicted on their

The sandy expanses of Banc d'Arguin's coastal waterways.

own. Of course, a serious depletion of the region's fish numbers would have a disastrous effect on the millions of birds which feed here during the winter months, building up their store of body fat before resuming their migratory flights. The over-fishing also threatens the livelihood of the Imraguen people, who have used traditional methods for subsistence fishing in these waters for generations.

Other threats to the bird colonies come from natural predators, such as the golden jackal, which ventures out to the smaller islands at low tide to feast.

The waters attract many sea mammals, such as orcas; porpoises; and five different varieties of dolphin, including the bottle-nosed dolphin. They arrive here in their hundreds during the seasonal mullet migration. But the most famous of all the park's resident marine animals is the monk seal: its colony of 100 to 150 individuals is the largest known concentration of this species - unusual in being the only one which can live in tropical conditions. Once found as far afield as the Black Sea, the monk seal was culled to near extinction on account of the value of its pelt and fat, which was used for making oil. More recently, Banc d'Arguin's monk seals suffered a blow from nature when the grottos they used for breeding suffered a cave-in, placing their future in some doubt.

AÏR AND TÉNÉRÉ
RESERVES

AIR AND TENERE
RESERVES

LOCATION

In the Air Mountains. The town of Iferouane lies on the western boundary, approximately centered at N 18° 40', E 08° 30'.

AREA

18,566,400ac (7,736,000ha).

FEATURES

The reserve comprises 6.1% of Niger and is a crucial habitat for the only remaining Sahelo-Saharan wildlife.

FLORA

• The vegetation of the basin areas is predominately Sahelian, including several species of acacia.
• In the wetter basin areas and some moist ravines high in the mountains are relicts of Sudanese forest, while wild olive trees are also found in the mountains.

FAUNA

• The increasingly rare addax, and the oryx are sometimes found within the reserve.
• Barbary sheep, now only found in small numbers, live in the mountains.

Barbary sheep.

A vast sea of sand: as far as the eye can see, enormous dunes rolling out over the horizon, shifting slowly but relentlessly through the timeless desert. The unyielding dunes of this desertscape are the closest thing you will see to waves if you visit this arid heart of northern Africa.

Although the Aïr and Ténéré Reserves are mainly desert, the mountains and basins shelter a surprising diversity of habitats. The expansive, rocky, and sparsely forested Aïr mountains cover approximately one fifth of the reserve and generate the precipitative conditions necessary to form the many Sahelian oases which are typical of the area. Up here, at altitudes of almost 6,600ft (2,000m), roam large animals such as ostrich, gazelles, baboons and antelopes. Some areas which are blessed with springs harbor plantations of olives and dates which are crammed onto the lower hillside terraces. It is in these mountains that some of our early ancestors have left their calling cards for posterity; with numerous rock paintings and carvings depicting scenes rich in wildlife, suggesting an unimagined fertility for the plains below which now cast their scorching sands asunder.

The vegetation of the basin areas includes several species of acacia. In the wetter basin areas and some moist ravines high in the mountains are relicts of Sudanese forest, while wild olive trees are also found in the mountains. The sand supports few trees but *Acacia tortilis* is capable of surviving the harsh environment. A very unusual, and important plant is the *Schouwia thebaica* the leaves of which are green and fleshy at the end of the cold season, providing crucial seasonal pasture.

At 18,566,400ac (7,736,000ha) the reserve comprises just over 6% of Niger and is a most important habitat for what remains of the characteristic Sahelo-Saharan wildlife. The increasingly rare addax, and the oryx are sometimes found within the reserve, visiting the wadis and grazing on seasonal and permanent pasture. Barbary sheep, now only found in small numbers, live in the mountains. There are many other threatened species in the park such as the dama, dorcas and slender-horned gazelles, and cheetah. Ostriches, heavily poached elsewhere, are found in healthy numbers, as are the predatory species including

FACILITIES

There is good potential for tourism, but there are no facilities at present. There is a small laboratory. Staff include a director, five foresters, three drivers, one guide, one mechanic, and two Peace Corps biologists. The IUCN/WWF Field Headquarters are at Iferouane.

(ABOVE) A Tuareg village within the reserve.

caracal, striped hyena, golden jackal, fennec, Ruppell's sand fox, and the sand cat.

Traditional hunting is actively pursued within the reserve, but has no major impact on the area. These traditional hunters take a few Barbary sheep every year but their effect on the population is probably negligible. Cheetah are often hunted as they are accused of stock damage, which leads to the biggest problem the area faces: pressure from the activities of the local people - semi-nomadic pastoralists raising camels, sheep and goats. The combination of drought in the late 1960s, 1970s and early 1980s and over-utilization of acacia trees by browsing livestock of the nomads, has degraded some areas very badly. This form of exploitation tends to be intensive. Strychnine is often used to kill jackals and hyenas, and as a consequence, other animals are killed as well. The Wildlife Department in Niger has recently issued a strong statement on the use of strychnine, reiterating that its use is illegal without authorization from the wildlife authority and other authorities concerned with natural resources.

These local people are virtually all Tuaregs, (of Berber origin) and there are approximately 2,500 within the reserve. Many of them have been fighting a rebellion against the government over the last few years. The Tuaregs recognize certain trees for their fruit-bearing potential - for example *Acacia albida* and *Acacia tortilis* - and they are specially protected. There is a respect for certain animals, such as the ostrich which are not hunted.

Unfortunately, the influx of people from different areas are breaking the traditions. Several generations ago a highly revered religious leader of one of the Sherifan tribes pronounced that no-one should cut trees, harm gazelles or kill ostriches. As a result a wadi area has been protected by this edict.

The reserve has suffered badly in recent years from fighting between the government forces of Niger and Mali, as well as from the Tuareg rebellion. It has been placed on the List of World Heritage in Danger at the request of the government.

A management plan, sponsored by the IUCN and the WWF, has been put in place to help conserve the endangered large mammals of the entire Sahelo-Saharan region, particularly the addax, scimitar-horned oryx, Barbary sheep and several species of gazelle. The project's long term objective is to rehabilitate the arid land fauna and flora to provide adequate living conditions to the local people and nomads. The field trips associated with the development of the reserve and subsequent analysis of data, have provided technicians from Niger with valuable training in ecological survey, practical conservation and game management, skills that will be in great demand in the future.

DJOUDJ
BIRD SANCTUARY

Located in a low-lying saline delta in the west African state of Senegal, this national bird sanctuary is one of the most important in the world, supporting, despite its relatively small size of 38,400ac (16,000ha), over three million aquatic birds from September to April. Djoudj occupies only part of the immense Senegal River Delta, and is the first fresh water stop for migratory birds after a long dry passage across the Sahara. The Djoudj Bird Sanctuary is able to retain large amounts of fresh water thanks to a system of dykes, built decades ago, which entirely surrounds it. Even in the dry season, when salinity is high, it is still the wettest area in the region, although the water during this period can become quite brackish.

It is nearly impossible to imagine the scenes at Djoudj when the migratory birds are there. The sight of the birds spread out along the shallows for literally miles is both glorious and surreal, reminiscent of the acres of tulips found in Holland in the spring: a repository of colors so brilliant and so vast that the eye has difficulty taking it all in. The noise of the birds is deafening yet touching, a rowdy affirmation of life, testifying to the completion of an enormous journey; proof of the waterfowls' vitality and amazing stamina. There is also a comicality to their cacophonous presence, with visitors detecting complaint, satisfaction, serenity and quarrelsomeness in their cries. Many days can be spent in fascination and amusement simply watching and listening to the birds.

The bird varieties are enormous, and include well-known species such as the flamingo, the spoonbill, the pelican, the cormorant, and the blue heron. Lesser-known species such as the Sudan bustard, the black-tailed godwit, the night heron, the fulvus tree duck, the white-faced tree duck, the spur-winged goose, and the African darter can also be found.

Recently, the mean annual precipitation in the sanctuary, which should be at least 10in (300mm), has been much less: sometimes as low as one fifth of the average. This alarming development could be due to long-term weather patterns which have not been monitored before; disruptions to the world's climate caused by natural activity such as volcanic eruption; or, quite possibly, the greenhouse effect. Whatever the cause, it poses a threat to the birds which depend on the sanctuary for fresh water and food. A dyke and dam system has already been put in place, ensuring that the park is not exposed to great fluctuations in water level. While this regulates the effects of flooding, it is far less effective when dealing with the complex problems created by prolonged drought.

Of course Djoudj National Bird Sanctuary has experienced dry spells before and the park management has tried to compensate for these. A temporary dam was built upriver at Kheune to act as a barrier against the movement of salt water from the delta up into the Senegal River during the dry season. While preserving fresh water upriver, the dam had the unforseen effect of reducing the supply of fresh water into Djoudj. So in 1985 the park had to be connected by canal with the dam's fresh water supply. Thus paradoxically the dam both helps and hinders the bird sanctuary, a common occurrence whenever man steps in on nature's behalf.

As fresh water is scarce in the whole delta area, permanent dams are being constructed to control the Senegal River, including one at Diama, which among other things is supposed to ensure regular water levels at the bird sanctuary. Whether or not this actually happens depends on the broader question of weather patterns which are dictated by global behaviour such as the burning of fossil fuels and the loss of forest cover. No amount of planning can compensate for a series of failed wet seasons. Whatever the future brings, it seems unlikely that this unique bird sanctuary can ever be looked at again as anything but fragile at best, and at worst, endangered.

DJOUDJ BIRD SANCTUARY

LOCATION

In a low valley 10mi (15km) north of Ross-Bethio and about 37mi (60km) north-east of Saint-Louis on the Delta of the Senegal River, Region du Fleuve, in the extreme north of the country, N 16° 30', W 16° 10'.

AREA

38,400ac (16,000ha)

FEATURES

This national bird sanctuary is one of the most important in the world, supporting, despite its relatively small size, over three million aquatic birds from September to April.

FLORA

- Vegetation reflects a low rainfall on unfavorable soils, with Sahelien type savanna dominated by spiny bushes and acacias. Halophytic plants cover much of the area.

FAUNA

- The bird varieties include well-known species such as the flamingo; the spoonbill; the pelican; the cormorant; and the blue heron. Lesser-known species such as the Sudan bustard, the black-tailed godwit, the night heron, the fulvus tree duck, the white-faced tree duck, the spur-winged goose and the African darter.

- Mammals include warthog and West African manatee; several species of crocodile and gazelle have been successfully reintroduced into the area.

FACILITIES

Around 5,000 tourists are lucky enough to visit Djoudj National Bird Sanctuary every year, arriving at the peak viewing time, from November to April. There are hotels in the nearby settlement of St Louis, as well as a small museum, and two camps are located on the borders of the sanctuary itself. Bird observation platforms have been erected at twelve strategic locations inside the park, and visitors can also hire canoes, for a closer view of the birds. However, anyone taking a canoe should exercise caution as there are several species of crocodile within the park. The park is closed for three months of the year, to allow research, maintenance and management. Prospective visitors should check closing times in advance.

African darter.

NIOKOLO-KOBA
NATIONAL PARK

N iokolo Koba is a relatively flat region, with small lines of hills about 660ft (200m) high, separated by wide floodplains which become inundated during the rains. The park is large enough - at 3,300sqmi (8,500sqkm) this is the largest protected area in western Africa - to support naturally sustaining populations of fauna and flora. This is one of the rare areas in Africa, for example, where the elephant population has been able to maintain itself without difficulty. Unfortunately this situation is under threat from poaching; a practice which has been, and remains, a serious threat to the park.

The plains, which are covered in herbaceous savannan foliage, provide grazing land for buffalo, giant eland, roan, and are also the haunt of lions.

Other carnivores which inhabit the area include leopard and hunting dog. The savanna area is relatively new, as it was formed mainly through controlled burning, a practice conducted by the former inhabitants of the park. It was a particularly destructive process which led to soil degradation and decreased the level of permanent vegetation. Many of the animals that now live in the park, however, rely on the savanna foliage for food, so current park management practices include controlled burning to preserve savanna areas. There are many seasonally flooded areas, which become completely inundated during the wet season from June to October. The areas of dry Sudanian forest in much of the park are alleviated by patches of bamboo.

NIOKOLO-KOBA NATIONAL PARK

LOCATION
Lying across the border between the adminis-trative regions of Sénégal-Oriental and La Casamance, on the River Gambia, close to the Guinea border in south-eastern Senegal, N 12° 30' to 13° 20', W 12° 20' to 13° 35'.

AREA
8,500sqkm (3,300sqmi).

FEATURES
This is the largest protected area in western Africa: its size enables it to support naturally sustaining populations of fauna and flora.

(ABOVE) A young chimpanzee.

FLORA

- As well as seasonally flooded grass plains of paspalum arbiculare and echinchloa, there are many areas in the park where semi-aquatic species of plants grow;- marshes, sand beds, river banks and the edges of ponds. Marsh foliage ranges from the thorny mimosa pigra to the wild rice oryza brachiyantha.

FAUNA

- There are about 80 species of mammal, 36 reptiles, 20 amphibians, and 60 species of fish recorded, as well as numerous invertebrates.
- The 330 species of birds in the park include raptors, such as Denham's bustard and the bateleur eagle, and many species of water birds such as the white-faced tree duck and the spur-winged goose.

FACILITIES

There is a luxury hotel at Simenti, which is the most visited part of the park. There are also bungalows and an hotel at Niokolo-Koba, lodgings at Badi, and several camping grounds. Animals can be viewed from hides or on guided safaris. Many animals disperse in the rains, so best viewing times are from the end of October to the end of June, when most tours are organized. There is an airstrip at Simenti.

A bateleur eagle taking off.

To the south, towards the Guinean border where the climate is more equatorial, there are patches of gallery forest. Chimpanzees tend to prefer these wetter forests. Other primates in the park include both patas and green monkey, bay colobus and guinea baboon. The 330 species of birds in the park include raptors, such as Denham's bustard and the bateleur eagle, and many species of water birds such as the white-faced tree duck and the spur-winged goose. The boundary to the park in the south-east and north-west is the Gambia river. In the river and its tributaries live three species of crocodile - Nile, slender-snouted and dwarf - and four species of tortoise. Hippopotami are often seen in the three major water courses within the park.

The main water courses comprise the River Gambia and its two tributaries, Niokolo Koba and Koulountou. These are the arteries of the park, providing the variation in moisture which creates much of the variation in the park's flora. There is an enormous range of plant species: at least 1,500 species are known to exist within the park. Vegetation changes with the most subtle differences in humidity, elevation and soil composition. As well as expanses of seasonally flooded grass plains, there are many areas of marshes, sand beds and river banks where semi-aquatic species grow. Marsh foliage ranges from the thorny Mimosa pigra to wild rice. Annuals grow on the seasonally flooded sandy river beds, and semi-aquatic species

fringe the banks. Some ponds are surrounded by dry foliage of either forest or grassland whereas others provide a moister habitat.

There is a general plan in place for the restoration of natural ecosystems within the park. Poaching is a serious problem: in the early 80's, the World Wide Fund for Nature supplied a Land Rover and several radios to be used in the combat against elephant poaching. The numbers of leopard and elephant in the park have decreased because of poaching over a number of years and there are few, if any, leopards left.

The park is under threat in several other areas, including dams planned for the Gambia and Niokola-Koba rivers, the building of an artificial lake and an increase in accessibility associated with industrial exploration such as mining and quarrying. When the park was first established, it was inhabited by people practising agriculture, cattle rearing, and some hunting. Bush fires were used to control the vegetation which resulted in degraded soils, the emergence of savanna vegetation, and the disappearance of large animals in some areas. However, all inhabitants were relocated outside the park area in the early 70's, although areas outside and within the park are still burnt.

- Also found are eland, red and grey duiker, and more occasionally, elephant and buffalo.
- The most common bird to be seen at high altitudes is the raven, but lammergeier, hillchat and scarlet tufted malachite sunbird are also sometimes seen.
- In the montane forest, three species of primate are to be found: the blue monkey, the black and the white colobus.
- There are many species which are endemic to the region, including the Abbott's duiker, the Abbot's starling, and the Kilimanjaro swallowtail butterfly.

FACILITIES

The national park has been developed with tourism in mind, and approximately 67,000 people visit each year. Visitors are allowed to climb to 13,200ft (4,000m) without a guide. Permission from the Chief Warden is necessary for climbing to the summit, and is restricted mainly to the organized four to five night climb to Kibo via the Marangu route which stops at Mandara, Horombo and Kibo huts: food, bedding and porters are provided. The summit can be reached by any reasonably fit person. The starting point at Marangu (30mi - 48km from Moshi and 52mi - 90km from Kilimanjaro International Airport) has hotel and hostel accommodation.

there has been evidence of a decrease in this water flow, most likely attributable to the changes in land use.

Above 15,200ft (4,600m), very few plants are able to survive the severe conditions, although mosses and lichens, species critical to the mountain's ability to retain rainfall, are found right up to the summit. Below the summit, heath and scrub plants struggle along the slopes, keeping close to the ground. Grasses also grow here, particularly in the wet hollows which litter the slopes. In these 'alpine bogs' are also found groundsel and Lobelia deckenii. Two unusual types of giant groundsel grow on the upper mountain slopes, one of which is endemic to Kilimanjaro. On the flatter areas which spread out below the upper moorland and above the forest there are more varieties of grasses as well as some bushes. Because the winds are mainly from the southeast, the south slopes are much moister than the north. The forests on the southern slopes are dominated by camphorwood and a rich understorey of tree and long spiked ferns, whereas the drier northern slopes support mostly cedar and olives.

Quite a few mammals are found at the higher altitudes above the tree line but it is likely that many of these are based in the lower forest habitats. Evidence is growing that several large mammal populations are under serious threat of local extinction, a fate that has already befallen the mountain reedbuck and the klipspringer. Rodents are particularly common, as are insects. Eland, red and grey duiker, and more occasionally, elephant and buffalo are often found grazing. The most common bird to be seen at high altitudes is the raven, but lammergeier, hillchat and scarlet tufted malachite sunbird are occasionally seen. In the montane forest, three species of primate are to be found: the blue and black monkeys, and the white colobus. Kilimanjaro tree hyrax and leopard are found in the park. The black rhinoceros was also once found, but this endangered animal has now disappeared from the forests of Kilimanjaro. There are many species which are endemic to the region, including the Abbott's duiker, the Abbot's starling, the Kilimanjaro swallowtail butterfly and its subspecies atavus which is found only on the mountain itself.

As in many other parks and reserves in Africa, resources are stretched, and manpower and equipment is not sufficient for full implementation of management in the area. Most difficulties are

(ABOVE) A giant lobelia.

(RIGHT) Elands at water.

encountered in the management and protection of the montane forest, with illegal hunting, honey gathering, tree felling, fuel wood collection, grass burning and incursions by domestic livestock, particularly in the south-west. Both honey gathering and grass burning result in outbreaks of uncontrolled fires every year, particularly during the dry season. As with moorland in many parts of the world, fire is almost certainly one of the major ecological factors that has influenced the mountain biota for hundreds of years, and management (or non-management) of fire is likely to continue presenting problems. Concern has been expressed that the frequency of fire on the Shira Plateau is increasing, and that this might pose a threat to the populations of giant groundsel. Problems also result from the heavy use of the area by tourists. The forest buffer zone is being maintained in six corridors within the park, but elsewhere felling has continued, and there has been some replacement with commercial plantations or maize crops.

NGORONGORO
CONSERVATION AREA

NGORONGORO CONSERVATION AREA

LOCATION

In the Arusha Region of Northern Tanzania, south-east of Serengeti National Park, S 02° 30′ to 03° 30′, E 34° 50′ to 35° 55′.

AREA

809,440ha (1,942,700ac).

FEATURES

Ngorongoro Crater is one of the largest inactive, unbroken and unflooded calderas in the world. It has a mean diameter of 10 to 12mi (16 to 19km), and a floor area of 62,400ac (26,000ha), with a rim wall which extends 1,320 to 2,010ft (400 to 610m) above the crater floor.

FLORA

- The remains of a dense montane forest are intermingled with scrub heath on the steep slopes.
- The crater floor is an open grassland with both brackish and fresh water lakes and swamp areas.
- There are two patches of acacia woodland, Lerai forest and Laiyanai forest.

Climbing the sides of this ancient volcano up to the crest of the rim, some 6,000ft (1,800m) above sea level, you have little idea just what you are about to behold. Peering down into the enormous crater, some 2,010ft (610m) below, through the haze you can make out countless tiny black dots. A confusing site, until you realize that the dots are in fact thousands of wildebeest, eland, zebra and gazelle grazing on the grassy crater floor. This is one of Africa's largest conglomerations of wildlife - an estimated 25,000 animals populate the 62,400ac (26,000ha) floor. One of the largest inactive, unbroken and unflooded calderas in the world, Ngorongoro's diameter ranges up to 12mi (19km). Lake Empakaai, and Olduvai Gorge are also within the conservation area. Towering above the craters are the volcanic massifs of Loolmalasin and Oldeani.

As a result of the variation in climate and land form there are three distinct habitats in the conservation area. The remains of a dense montane forest are intermingled with scrub heath on the steep slopes. The crater floor is an open grassland with both brackish and fresh water lakes and swamp areas. And there are two patches of acacia woodland, Lerai forest and Laiyanai forest. The grasses and shrubs of the plains, although able to support large numbers of animals, become almost deserts in times of drought.

The large numbers of herbivores in turn support carnivores. The crater boasts the densest known population of lions, and cheetahs, leopards and hyenas are also found roaming. There are some black rhinoceros, possibly one of the only remaining viable breeding populations, while hippopotami are also occasionally found. Buffalo, elephant, and mountain reedbuck graze on the crater rim. The plains are also mainly inhabited by wildebeest, while waterbuck keep to the area of the Lerai forest. Hartebeest and spotted hyena are found throughout the reserve. Both the wild dog and golden cat have recently declined, in some places within the reserve to the point of non-existence. The bird life in the reserve is rich.

Ostriches and the kori bustard are also found on the reserve, as are the Egyptian vulture, Verreaux's eagle, and the lesser flamingo. The forests have many species of the colorful sunbird.

About 22,000 nomadic Maasai live in the reserve accompanied by ten times as many grazing livestock. There is, however, no one inhabiting the craters or the forest. The reserve was first established as a conservation area for the Maasai people. The government of Tanzania is attempting to balance the interests of the Maasai people and the conservation of the environment, but is faced with many serious problems. About 5% of the area has been degraded by trampling and overgrazing.

- Wild ungulates in the crater include wildebeest, zebra, eland, and gazelle.
- There are some black rhinoceros, possibly one of the only remaining viable breeding populations.
- The crater boasts the densest known population of lions.
- Buffalo, elephant, and mountain reedbuck graze on the crater rim where the leopard prowls.
- The plains are also mainly inhabited by wildebeest, while waterbuck keep to the area of the Lerai forest.
- Ostriches and the kori bustard are also found on the reserve, as are the Egyptian vulture, Verreaux's eagle, and the lesser flamingo. The forests have many species of the colorful sunbird. The Kilimanjaro swallowtail butterfly also inhabits the area.

FACILITIES

There are three lodges on the crater rim and one at Ndutu, and vehicles and guides can be hired from the authority to go into the crater. The only interpretive center is at Olduvai, which is focused on the interpretation of the Gorge and its excavations. About 24% of all tourists visiting the parks of northern Tanzania stop at Ngorongoro. Visitor numbers are increasing substantially.

There is poaching, mainly of black rhinoceros and leopards. Wildebeest have increased to 1.3 million which is problematic in that they carry malignant catarrh fever, which kills cattle. The forests to the north-east are increasingly threatened by fuel wood gathering, both by people living in the conservation area and others from villages in the Karatu and Kitete areas along the eastern boundary. A number of poorer Maasai from the conservation area make a living collecting honey from wild bee colonies in the forest, frequently burning trees in the process.

The forest areas of the reserve are essential as they protect and preserve the water catchment, as

Zebras and wildebeests grazing on the crater floor.

well as the soil and other vegetation. Cultivation is not allowed in the area. The reserve provides a space where the indigenous inhabitants, and the wildlife, can live as they have always lived, in relative harmony with nature, but it is not easy to maintain this harmony in the midst of the many and radical changes which are shaking and shaping the globe.

Wildebeests flee a
waterhole with a
lioness in hot pursuit.

A herd of African elephants roam Ngorongoro.

SELOUS
GAME RESERVE

A mother giraffe and her young.

SELOUS GAME RESERVE

LOCATION

South-east Tanzania, S 07° 17' to 10° 15', E 36° 04' to 38° 46'.

AREA

19,500sqmi (50,000sqkm).

FEATURES

Selous Game Reserve is the second largest game reserve in Africa.

FLORA

- There is a variety of vegetation with patches of dense thicket, riverine and groundwater forest, 2,000 species of plant have been recorded.

FAUNA

- Animals include giraffe, zebra, waterbuck, cheetah, buffalo, impala, wildebeest, elephant, crocodile, hippos and sable antelope.

FACILITIES

The reserve is accessible by air or by the Tazara railway. There are three tented camps (one luxury) and a bungalow-style hotel along the Rufiji River in a tourist area where hunting is prohibited except for meat supply for the camps.
The reserve is inaccessible during the rainy season (March to May).

Selous Game Reserve, with an enormous expanse of 19,500sqmi (50,000sqkm), is the second largest and one of the oldest game reserves in Africa. The decision was made when the reserve was established to evacuate the local human population and the resulting decrease in hunting and other forms of encroachment has allowed Selous to evolve into one of Africa's last great areas of wilderness, where the bush stands untamed and the large herds of wild beasts thrive, unmolested by human interference.

There are two main vegetation types in the reserve. To the east is sparsely wooded grasslands, but by far the larger area of the park is deciduous miombo woodland, a unique type of forest and one which is believed to be maintained through fire. The temperate weather and abundance of water has created a variety of different vegetation with patches of dense thicket, riverine and groundwater forest scattered throughout the park and along the waterways. Although the soil is poor, 2,000 species of plant have been recorded, and a comprehensive survey has yet to be made.

This relatively sparse vegetation supports a wealth of wildlife. Grassland animals include giraffe, zebra, waterbuck, warthog, and cheetah. There are particularly high numbers of buffalo, impala, wildebeest, elephant, crocodile, hippopotamus and sable antelope. However, despite management of hunting, animals such as the elephant and the sable antelope, both of which live in the miombo woodland, and the black rhinoceros and sassaby antelope, are declining rapidly in numbers.

Poaching, mostly commercial, is a problem and there is a lack of funds with which to deal with it. No forest exploitation has taken place and mineral exploration has as yet failed to find any valuable deposits. A serious threat is the proposed Stiegler's Gorge Dam Project intended to harness the flood waters of the Rufiji River. Both dam and reservoir would be entirely within the reserve and cover some 106,000ac (44,000ha). Seismic roads for oil exploration are being built into 75% of the reserve. The main threat is increased accessibility to the area and the presence of a population within the reserve to maintain these developments.

Because of the difficulties of transportation, the interior of Selous is seldom patrolled, and the most immediate threat to wildlife is commercial poaching for meat and trophies. As is often the case with damaging amounts of poaching, the problem is not with the local inhabitants so much as with commercial poachers and foreign buyers. Communal wildlife management programs, designed to involve the local community in the management of natural resources, is intended to stem poaching and is regarded as a more effective control than increased policing. These programs have been very successful in regard to the local management of natural resources, but have not been able to solve the external threats.

SERENGETI
NATIONAL PARK

Serengeti is easily the most renowned wildlife park on earth. Within its 5,800sqmi (14,763sqkm) are more than three million large mammals living in total freedom on the 'endless plains' - the meaning of 'Serengeti' in the local Maasai language. Every May/June, the annual migration starts, and hundreds of thousands of wild game, led by wildebeest, start to move across the plains to new grazing grounds. These enormous herds race westwards, howling as they go, so that the air reverberates with an almighty roar accompanied by clouds of dust. Lines of wildebeest up to 25mi (40km) long have been observed on occasions.

The plains themselves consist of a thin layer of volcanic ash over crystalline rock. It is a fragile basis for plant life and prone to drought. The dominant vegetation in this arid environment is couch grass. Sedges surround the few lakes and waterholes that exist. Amongst the grasses, granite rock outcrops point to the sky, seemingly in supplication, praying for rain. The lifeline of the Serengeti is its two rivers which are seasonally filled from November through to May with 48in (1210mm) of rainfall annually. There is a large area of acacia woodland in the center of the park and a more densely wooded area in the hills to the north with some gallery forest.

Apart from the spectacularly large herds of wildebeest, zebra, giraffe, buffalo, waterbuck, and Thomson's gazelle which move through the park migrating between seasonal water supplies, there are also black rhinos, hyrax, sitatunga, several species of mongoose, primates, otters and many species of rodents and bats. Predators found in the park, also in abundance, are lions, spotted hyena, hunting dog, leopard, cheetah, golden and side striped jackals, and smaller predators such as the bat-eared fox and ratel. More than 350 species of bird have been recorded. There are particularly high numbers of raptors, 34 species, including six types of vulture and the kori bustard. There are also many smaller birds which are only found in limited areas, such as the rufous-tailed weaver.

Bat-eared fox.

The park has been well utilized for scientific research with much valuable work having been done on animal behavior, the ecological effects of burning, climate variability and vegetation. Serengeti is free of human habitation, a state which is continually being reaffirmed, as there has been some human encroachment and cultivation on the west and north-west borders. The woodlands are particularly vulnerable to damage from elephants, fires, firewood collection, as well as the encroachment of cultivation. This damage is further exacerbated by giraffes grazing on new shoots and forest regrowth. Poaching, particularly in the corridor areas, is difficult to control without adequate resources. Most of the parks in Africa face problems of poaching and increasing numbers of uncontrollable fires. Many projects have been set up in the park to deal with just these issues but as always there is a lack of funds, both for further control of these problems and for the necessary further research into environmental conservation and management.

SERENGETI NATIONAL PARK

LOCATION

West of Great Rift Valley, 80mi (130km) west-north-west of Arusha, in Mara, Arusha, and Shinyanga regions,
S 01° 30' to 03° 20',
E 34° 00' to 35° 15'.

AREA

5,800sqmi (14,763sqkm).

FEATURES

Serengeti is easily the most renowned wildlife park on earth. Every year around May/June, hundreds of thousands of wild game start to move across the plains to new grazing grounds. Lines of wildebeest up to 25mi (40km) long have been observed on occasions.

FLORA

• The dominant vegetation in this arid environment is couch grass. Sedges surround the few lakes and waterholes that exist.
• There is a large area of acacia woodland in the center of the park and a more densely wooded area in the hills to the north with some gallery forest.

A thundering herd of wildebeest leap down a cliff along the Mara river.

(ABOVE) For the first few months the cheetah cub's fur is fluffy from head to tail.

(LEFT) Spotted hyena.

(FAR LEFT) An African spoonbill with its newly won meal - a very tasty frog.

A flock of white backed vultures feasting on a zebra.

ICHKEUL
NATIONAL PARK

ICHKEUL NATIONAL PARK

LOCATION

In northern Tunisia, approximately 19mi (30km) south-west of the Mediterranean coast, N 37° 10', E 09° 40'.

AREA

30,240ac (12,600ha); the lake area varies with season; minimum area of 25,900ac (10,775ha) to a maximum of 30,200ac (12,600ha) in the rainy season.

FEATURES

'Lac Ichkeul' is the sole surviving remnant of an ancient northern African lake chain. Today it plays a crucial role as a stopover point for thousands of migrating birds.

FLORA

- Of particular importance are the numerous beds of Potamogeton pectinatus which is a major source of food for the many species of bird in the wetlands.

- The park has a typically semi-arid climate dominated by Mediterranean-type plant species.

- The mountain and its foothills are dominated by a covering of lentisc with wild olive and phillyrea.

'Lac Ichkeul' is the sole surviving remnant of an ancient northern African lake chain. Today it plays a crucial role as a stopover point for thousands of migrating birds. It is an enormous body of water, comprising 20,400ac (8,500ha) of lake habitat in which salt and fresh water meet. The lake's connection with the sea is indirect, as it joins the marine lagoon 'Lac de Bizerte' through the river 'Oued Tindja'. Several rivers pour fresh water into the west and south of the lake, and fresh water fish and vegetation are found in these areas. The lake is greatly affected by seasonal changes; in summer the fresh water rivers dry up and rainfall is minimal. With this evaporation of water in the summer heat, the salinity reaches extremely high levels; after the first autumn rains it falls again. The annual rainfall for the area is quite low, but with the drainage of the rivers the amount of rainwater which enters the lake each year is very high.

The lake is rich in vegetation. Of particular importance are the numerous beds of *Potamogeton pectinatus* which is a major source of food for the many species of bird in the wetlands - especially the water fowl. These beds are breeding grounds for many animals. The park has a typically semi-arid climate dominated by Mediterranean-type plant species. Distinct habitats within the park include the mountain and its foothills, dominated by a covering of lentisc with wild olive and phillyrea. There is a rich variety of northern Tunisian plant species. The vegetation of the marshes and open water areas is varied and luxuriant. The threatened *Ranunculus ophioglossum*, recorded at only a few sites in Tunisia, also grows in the marshes.

Ichkeul wetland is one of the most important sites in the entire Mediterranean region for wintering Palearctic waterfowl, with records of up to 400,000 birds present at one time. More than 185 species of bird have been recorded. The most numerous species recorded are wigeon, pochard and coot. The high records for greylag goose indicate that Ichkeul is the most important wintering station in the Maghreb for this species.

Up to 600 of the threatened white-headed duck, 4% of the known world population, have been observed. Additional wetland birds found include mallard, high numbers of teal, pintail, shoveler and black-winged stilt. Other species include the booted eagle, Bonelli's eagle, peregrine falcon, and collared pratincole. There are large numbers of migrant and resident marsh harrier and reed warbler. There are migrant white stork and records of the uncommon black stork and glossy ibis. The purple gallinule breeds in the dense reeds.

One of the most notable of the mammals recorded at Ichkeul is the otter. Less than ten animals are believed to occur. There are large populations of wild boar, European genet, as well as a limited number of crested porcupine, mongoose and Asiatic water buffalo, which was introduced at an early period of Tunisian history.

In the center of the lake is the 'Djebel Ichkeul'. This limestone massif possesses extremely rich deposits of fossils from the tertiary, quaternary and Pleistocene periods, the latter of which

FAUNA

- Ichkeul wetland is one of the most important sites in the entire Mediterranean region for wintering Palearctic waterfowl.
- More than 185 species of bird have been recorded, including numerous wigeon, pochard and coot. The high records for greylag goose indicate that Ichkeul is the most important wintering station in the Maghreb for this species.
- Up to 600 of the threatened white-headed duck, 4% of the known world population, have been observed.
- Additional wetland birds found include mallard, high numbers of teal, pintail, shoveler and black-winged stilt.
- One of the most notable of the mammals recorded at Ichkeul is the otter, less than ten animals are believed to occur. There are large populations of wild boar and European genet, as well as a limited number of crested porcupine, mongoose and Asiatic water buffalo.

FACILITIES

An extensive program promoting natural history tourism has resulted in a dramatic increase in tourist numbers. The visitor facilities, including audio-visual displays, small museum and library are situated on the northern slopes of the Djebel.

includes hominid and primate remains. It rises out of the quaternary lake basin and is home to wild boar, European genet, crested porcupine, mongoose and asiatic water buffalo. It is uncertain whether the water buffalo were introduced as recently as between 1837 and 1855, from Italy, or earlier in Carthaginian times. The buffalo population was greatly reduced in 1954 when most were slaughtered for food, but with the aid of breeding programs their numbers have increased. Vegetation on the massif varies from a dense coverage of lentisc, phillyrea and wild olive to looser associations.

This valuable and magnificent meeting place of water, land and sea has been harshly treated. Cultivation around the park's fringes is heavy and run off of fertilizers and pesticides threatens the life of the lake. The damming of the Djoumine and Rhezla rivers has increased salinity. And the mining of stone and marble in the recent past, from a quarry on the southern slope of Djebel Ichkeul, has also greatly effected the water content of the lake,

A white-headed duck displaying in courtship.

damaging plant and animal life. Illegal occupation and grazing of cattle sheep and goats on the massif has contributed to a damaged eco-system and threatens the population of water buffalo.

With the official recognition of Lac Ichkeul as a wetland of international importance - as a destination of migratory birds and for its unique habitats on land and water - steps have been taken to lessen the damaging effects of human activity on the environment. As well as measures to decrease grazing and restrictions on hunting and fishing, studies into the maintenance of water purity and freshness have been undertaken. Plans have included a sluice on the Oued Tindja to restrict the flow of salt water in an attempt to balance the lack of fresh water which is a direct result of human interference. The wetlands have managed thus far to adjust to changes and with a little help they may survive with much of their integrity intact.

GARAMBA
NATIONAL PARK

GARAMBA
NATIONAL PARK

LOCATION

In Uele District, north-east Zaïre, on the Sudan border contiguous in the north-east to Lantoto, N 03° 45' to 04° 41', E 28° 48' to 30° 00'.

AREA

1,180,800ac (492,000ha).

(ABOVE) A leopard savours its prey.

Located in north-east Zaire, Garamba National Park is surrounded on three sides by Zairian hunting reserves which total more than 6,250sqmi (10,000sqkm), forming an immense buffer zone for the park proper; while in the north, it shares a border with Sudan's Lantoto Game Reserve. Dating back to 1938, Garamba currently covers 1,180,800ac (492,000ha).

There are several different terrains in Garamba, ranging from the densely wooded savanna, papyrus marshes and forests in the north and west, which give way in the center to more open bush savanna with clumps of dense woods. This then merges with the huge savanna grasslands which makes up a majority of the park. These grasslands are dissected by numerous small rivers with valley grasslands and papyrus swamps. Grass height ranges up to 17ft (5m): a potential cause of catastrophe should a large-scale fire ever break out, particularly during the dry season, from November to March, when temperatures can reach 100°F (40°C) and hot, very dry north-easterly winds sweep the countryside.

The park's great importance lies in the fact that it harbors the world's last natural population of northern white rhinoceros, also known as the square-lipped rhinoceros. In 1960 there were over 1,000 of these extraordinary animals roaming free in Garamba. In 1984 there were 15. This shocking reduction in population has led the IUCN - World Conservation Union to place the white northern rhino on its list of the 12 most endangered animals on earth.

Poaching alone is responsible for threatening the northern white rhinoceros with extinction. The horn of the rhino (actually an outgrowth of skin and cartilage with no core of bone) is highly prized in four countries: China; Taiwan; Hong Kong; and Yemen. A fifth country, North Korea, has also been linked to this illegal trade: allegedly using diplomatic pouches to move the horn through airports.

In Yemen, the horn is used for fashioning handles for ornamental daggers. In China, the horn is falsely believed to have medical properties, particularly the ability to reduce fever. In Taiwan and Hong Kong the horn is revered as a sovereign aphrodisiac, because of its supposed likeness to the erect penis. Wealthy businessmen from Taiwan in particular are willing to pay vast sums for the horn: as much as $US 132,000 per pound.

Although Britain, like most nations, is supposed to be enforcing a ban on the sale of rhino horn, a recent survey revealed that over half of Hong Kong's pharmacies openly sold products either made from rhino horn, or claiming to be made from rhino horn. And it has been alleged that Chinese authorities in the seventies and eighties bought up huge quantities of rhino horn, mainly off-cuts from Yemen, because it was viewed as an excellent hedge against inflation. With so many buyers, and so much official indifference, no wonder the rhino population suffered such a drastic decline, and in poverty-stricken Zaire, the potential rewards were simply too great to resist.

The slaughter of rhinoceroses is a highly-organized and bloody operation. Helicopters, automatic weapons and even light canons have all been used to hunt rhinos. When a rhino is brought down, its horns are removed as quickly as possible, usually with buzz saws and often while the animal is still alive. Anyone stumbling onto such a scene,

whether they be park rangers, local inhabitants or tourists, risks being murdered; the poachers showing as much mercy to potential witnesses as they do to their prey. In the 1970's and 1980's, local poachers were assisted by combatants from the civil wars in Sudan and Uganda, who either participated personally in the slaughter, or else made weapons and transport available to the locals.

Because the home range of a rhino can vary anywhere from 10 to 40 square miles, it's exceedingly hard to keep track of Garamba's remaining population. Both aerial and ground censuses have been carried out and five new lookout/patrol posts have been built. Shifts are organized so that at any one time there are two eight-men patrols in rhino country. The number of guards has been increased to 190, and they now receive proper training, better pay, and are armed with automatic rifles that allow them to compete with the advanced weaponry of the poachers. These new measures have been effective, as rhino poaching has been all but eliminated over the last few years in Garamba. As a result the rhino population is increasing and Garamba has now been taken off the List of World Heritage in Danger.

Unfortunately, Garamba's impressive herds of elephants have suffered a similar fate to the northern white rhinoceros, especially during two particularly lethal periods: the early 1960's, when Zaire was in political and social turmoil; and the 1970's and early 1980's, when the rhino horn and ivory markets really took off. Garamba's elephant population in the mid-seventies was well over 16,000. Today it's around 4,000.

Also present in the park are leopards, roan antelope, bush pigs, warthogs, hippopotamus, buffalo, hartebeest, kob, waterbuck, olive baboon, colobus, vervet, golden cat, lion, chimpanzees in the forested areas, and northern savanna giraffe, found nowhere else in Zaire.

Garamba is famous for its African Elephant Domestication Center in the south-west of the park. Here elephants are studied, and trained to carry tourists on safari. It is part of an attempt to develop tourism that involves local people living on the fringes of the park. But there is something undeniably sad about the notion of elephants carrying tourists through countryside where they once roamed freely and in numbers.

FLORA

Terrains range from densely wooded savanna, papyrus marshes and forests, to more open bush savanna with clumps of dense woods, to huge savanna grasslands which makes up a majority of the park.

FAUNA

Present in the park are northern white rhinoceros, leopards, roan antelope, bush pigs, warthogs, hippopotamus, buffalo, hartebeest, kob, waterbuck, olive baboon, colobus, vervet, golden cat, lion, chimpanzees in the forested areas, elephants, and northern savanna giraffe.

FACILITIES

Accommodation is available at Nagero, the head station of the park, and Gangala-na-Bodio, the second station, where the African Elephant Domestication Center is located. The construction of new roads, and the development of river transport and crossings, together with the elephant-back safaris, makes Garamba an extremely accessible national park to visit. There are plans to greatly enhance tourist facilities in the near future.

KAHUZI-BIEGA
NATIONAL PARK

KAHUZI-BIEGA
NATIONAL PARK

LOCATION

Eastern Zaïre, (31mi)
50km west of the town
of Bukavu in Kivu
Region, near the
Rwanda and Burundi
borders,
S 02° 10' to 02° 52',
E 28° 40' to 28° 50'.

AREA

1,440,000ac
(600,000ha).

FEATURES

This park's most famous
inhabitants are its
colony of 200 to 300
mountain gorillas which
are mainly found in the
mountain forest at an
altitude of between
6,900 and 7,900ft
(2,100 and 2,400m),
but are also found in the
upper reaches of the
rainforest.

FLORA

- Two-thirds of the
  mountain forest is
  dense primary forest
  intermixed with
  bamboo, especially at
  higher altitudes.
- Some patches of
  more open vegetation
  occur at lower
  altitudes.
- The remaining area is
  mainly mesophytic
  woodland including
  Hagenia trees and
  areas of swamp and
  peatbog.
- Alpine and
  sub-alpine grassland
  occur at high
  altitudes.
- There is a vast
  undulating area of
  equatorial rainforest.

This park of 1,440,000ac (600,000ha) is named after two extinct volcanoes which lie within its boundaries, close to the borders of Rwanda and Burundi. The park was first established in 1970 and the area was expanded to its present size in 1975, with the addition of a vast area of equatorial rainforest. The rapid expansion of the park's size reflects the importance that was given to creating a buffer-zone to protect the habitat of its most famous inhabitants: Kahuzi-Biega's colonies of 200 to 300 mountain gorillas.

The park's altitude ranges up to 3,400m (11,000ft), located as it is in the western mountains of the Great Rift Valley in the Zaire River Basin. The terrain mainly consists of virgin mountain forest and alpine grassland. There are also substantial stands of bamboo at high altitudes, and an immense section of lower, equatorial rainforest.

The wildlife in the park is varied and rich primates include the mountain gorilla, chimpanzee, owl-faced monkey, and numerous cercopithecinae and colobinae, including black and white colobus monkey and red colubus. Other mammals include elephant, forest hog and many antelope and duiker. avifauna include the endemic Rockefeller's sunbird, African green broadbill, and grauer's swamp warbler.

The gorillas are mainly found in the mountain forest at altitudes up to 2,400m (7,900ft), but are also found in the upper reaches of the rainforest. These herbivores range over a surprisingly wide territory, favoring secondary forest to primary ones during the months of December to June. It is in the secondary forests, with their clearings and less-dense foliage, where the gorillas find plenty of accessible food as well as an abundance of material for creating their 'nests' - platforms made of sticks and twigs perched in trees.

Towards the end of the dry season, in July and August, the gorillas enter the primary forests, where the more humid conditions assure them of nourishment, although the density of the vegetation makes climbing even more difficult than it usually is, as they haul their enormous weights up the higher trees to reach their food. The park's chimpanzees are far better suited to life in these primary forests, as they are more adept climbers.

At the beginning of the wet season, in late September, the gorillas move into the bamboo stands, and a period of 'feasting' begins, lasting till mid-December, when the bamboo shoots are too hard to eat. They then return to the secondary forests, which, thanks to the rains, again contain a profusion of food, and the gorilla's annual cycle begins anew.

These magnificent animals, with their long, lustrous blue-black coats with its distinctive silver shadowing on the backs of the mature males, generally live in small colonies. Occasionally lone males will live on their own, after having failed to establish a 'family'. Gorillas have, to a certain extent, always been mythologized for their strength and power, and there are special tours arranged to parks like Kahuzi-Biega to capitalize on this. Unfortunately, many tourists are not satisfied with just visiting their natural habitat with the hope of perhaps catching a glimpse of them; they want photos to take home, as proof that they've 'done Africa'. As gorillas are relatively shy animals, spending most of their time in the woods, they don't easily lend themselves to being photographed. So some unscrupulous guides have taken to leading tourists to gorilla groups then deliberately provoking the animals. If the gorillas feel threatened enough, they will raise themselves on their legs to the sound of shutters in a show of territorial protection. Sometimes the males 'rush' the groups. That is, they raise their arms and make as if to attack. It is a menacing sight, provoked merely for the sake of a snapshot. Not only does this practice disturb the animals, it needlessly places both gorillas and tourists in a situation of potential danger.

The park's wardens do their best to try to educate tourists and to prevent such degrading scenes from occurring. It's easy to blame the guides for inciting such encounters, but of course the responsibility lies with the tourist, on whom the

while 84 species are found above the falls, including African mottled eel, tigerfish, kafue pike and silver barbel.

There has been quite a range of development within the park, much before its establishment. Some of the development associated with the power generation facilities is particularly intrusive. Particularly worrying is the proposal to construct a dam across Batoka Gorge, a move which would undoubtedly cause flooding within the park. Cattle grazing has become well established within the park boundaries, and there is gradual encroachment of small-scale cultivation of maize and sorghum. The town of Livingstone is expanding rapidly, and local people and businesses are not currently motivated towards nature conservation. The situation is perhaps exacerbated by insufficient funds and manpower available to the park authorities. The 'rainforest' is vulnerable to disturbance by trampling, which allows penetration by ruderal species such as lantana, and when grossly disturbed the forest cannot regenerate easily, giving way to xeric scrub.

The discovery of stone artefacts of Homo habilis near the falls dates the cultural history of the area back approximately three million years. Stone tools from the Middle Stone Age (approximately 50,000 years ago), as well as weapons, adornments and digging tools from the Late Stone Age (10,000 to 2,000 years ago), have been unearthed. That community appears to have been displaced about 2,000 years ago by Iron Age farmers, who used iron tools, kept livestock and lived in villages. Very little change occurred in the area until after the 'discovery' of the falls by David Livingstone in 1855. He gave the falls their name after Queen Victoria of England. Today a large bronze statue of Livingstone stares east along the line of the falls, opposite the spot where he was first taken to see them and where he is reputed to have said:

'Scenes so lovely must have been gazed upon by angels in their flight.'

Vervet monkey.

MANA POOLS, SAPI AND CHEWORE
RESERVES

The cold morning air moves quietly across the dark valley floor. Underneath the old gnarled acacias, long grasses dance lightly in the breeze in tune with the soft chattering of the waking birdlife. The night stillness of the river breaks into gentle ripples that run patiently across its surface, and as the darkness sheds its coat, the warm glow of the morning's rays reveal a wondrous sight. One by one they appear out of the blackness - as far as the eye can see - hundreds upon hundreds of mammals cover the valley floor, waking to another day's grazing in the mid-Zambezi Valley.

It is a staggering sight during the dry season; thousands of elephant, buffalo, eland, hippopotamus, sable, zebra, impala, waterbuck and black rhinoceros congregate around the shady water holes of the valley floor where grasses and browsing plants thrive much further into the dry season than they do in the rest of the valley. Once the wet season has finished, it doesn't take long for soil moisture levels to decline, and for the grasses and browsing plants to stop growing. It is then that the large migrations of browsing mammals from higher up in the valley and on the escarpment, down to the moister soils of the alluvial plains begins. Some of the browsers, such as the eland and the black rhinoceros, show less of a seasonal pattern in their movements, as they are able to obtain adequate food away from the alluvial system throughout the year - they tend to move into this area more often when they are in need of shade and water.

This World Heritage site comprises three separate and adjoining reserves - Mana Pools National Park, which is fully protected, and Sapi and Chewore Safari areas, where strictly controlled hunting is still allowed. The entire area covers almost 2,700sqmi (7,000sqkm), and over 4,700sqmi (12,000sqkm) when the adjoining buffer zones are included. Importantly, there is no permanent human habitation within the property. There are several striking features to the landscape, including the Zambezi escarpment, which rises up sharply some 3,300ft (1,000m) from the valley floor and forms the southern most limit. Mupata Gorge, some 19mi (30km) long, slices dramatically through the Chewore Mountains, with the Zambezi River flowing rapidly along the bottom of its steep sides.

Well grassed communities dominate the mountainous escarpment and higher Chewore areas. The valley floor is dominated by mopane woodlands or dry highly deciduous thickets known as jesse. Seasonal tributaries crossing the valley floor support extensive riparian communities.

A lot of the mammals are to be found grazing amongst the river terraces of the Mana Pools area. The dominant tree species on this open-wooded alluvial plain is the acacia albida, a plant of particular importance as it provides shade and fodder exclusively during the dry season. Its large protein rich pods are produced in quantities of up to 920 pounds per acre, providing a crucial food source for the large mammals. Once the water table starts to rise in the wet season, the larger mammals tend to move out, leaving the new growth largely to the invertebrates. However, some mammals do stay behind, including hippopotami, vervet monkeys and waterbuck.

Birdlife in the valley is particularly rich - the sand and pebble banks of the Zambezi provide numerous isolated breeding spots that are free of most predators. As a consequence, over 380 species are known in the area. The river also provides the ideal breeding environment for something much larger - the Nile crocodile. It is now thought that this is one of the most important crocodile populations in Central Africa, and special attention is therefore paid to their nurseries, which are most often located on sandy islands in midstream. In breeding season it is possible to view one of nature's more amazing sights - a huge crocodile cradling its young ever so gently in its mouth.

Natural seasonal flooding of low-lying areas was seriously curtailed by the completion of Kariba Dam in 1958 and these areas are further threatened by a proposed hydroelectric scheme at Mapata Gorge which would create a 204,000ac (85,000ha)

Greater kudu.

lake obliterating much of the Zambezi floodplain and halving the carrying capacity of Mana Pools. An environmental assessment is being completed. Other problems include poaching, especially of fish in the Zambezi, and destruction of habitats by elephants. The Harare/Lusaka main road passes through the area with associated settlements and there is a private estate on the Zambezi near Chirundu. The area is of limited agricultural potential and has never been used extensively for livestock grazing. The site is under further threat from proposed oil exploration of the Zambezi Valley, including within the national park's boundaries. Initial seismic investigations will require the construction of 'trace line' roads into the park, leading to erosion and ease of access for poachers.

One of the features of Mana Pools National Park is the unique opportunity it offers visitors to walk and camp in true African bushland. Here it is possible to view first hand and at close quarters the grace and majesty of the large African mammals as they wander freely, browsing, sleeping, drinking and lazily soaking up the warm African sun. As with many truly exciting experiences, walking in this area is not without its dangers, but these may be minimized by taking sensible precautions and taking the advice of the park rangers.

- One of the more important populations of Nile crocodile in Central Africa, more than 1,000 individuals.
- The most important population of black rhinoceros existing, more than 500 individuals.
- More than 380 bird species, including the African skimmer, white fronted sandplover, stilt, red winged pratincole, and lilian lovebird.

FACILITIES

This area provides opportunities to experience some of the greatest seasonal mammal concentrations in a natural environment. It is ensured that recreational hunting will not impair the essential wilderness qualities and resource values for future generations. The number of cars allowed into Mana Pools National Park at any one time is limited. Mana Pools is only partially developed as a tourist center, but is so popular that the available facilities are prone to saturation. There is a tourist camp at Chikwenya on the confluence of the Sapi and Zambezi Rivers, but there are no tarred roads and visitors are strictly confined. Visitors are allowed to walk in the riparian woodlands in the park.

ASIA

HUANGLONG

HUANGLONG

LOCATION

Songpan County, north-western Sichuan Province, in the southern part of the Min Shan Mountain Range, N 32° 37' to 32° 54', E 103°37' to 104° 08'.

AREA

148,200ac (60,000ha).

FEATURES

- Spectacular mountain scenery, including permanent snow fields, strange karst formations, plummeting valleys, and glaciers invest the region with a splendid isolation.
- Tectonic activity originally formed these vast peaks and precipitous valleys, and the region is still plagued by earthquakes.
- The altitude varies from 5,577ft (1,700m) at Fan Cave to 18,333ft (5,588m) at Snow Mountain Peak.
- The most famous individual sites are Danyun Gorge, its cliffs dropping to the Fujiang River, and 'Yellow Dragon Gully' with its limestone, multi-colored pools.

(PREVIOUS PAGE)
Siberian tiger.

This area remained untouched for centuries for two reasons: its inaccessibility, due to its altitude; and the great reverence and respect with which the area was treated, because of its strong religious associations with Tibetan Buddhism. Unfortunately this sense of sacredness was lost during the cataclysm of the Cultural Revolution in the 1960s, and it wasn't until 1987 that the site finally received official state protection from the Provincial Government of Sichuan.

The most sacred sites to be found in Huanglong include the Body Washing Falls, a cascade which is believed to have miraculous properties, such as the power to bestow fertility; twin stone pagodas at the Jade Bathing Ponds, which mark the burial site of the grandson of the founder of the Tang Dynasty; two temples, one of which is in ruins, at Huanglong; and a cave thought to have once been inhabited by a wise Taoist hermit.

Located in the southern section of the Min Shan mountain range, the site possesses truly spectacular mountain scenery, which includes perpetually snow-covered peaks, plummeting valleys, and glaciers. The area is troubled by earthquakes, resting as it does on the Snow Mountain Great Fault. Indeed it was tectonic activity which originally formed these vast peaks and precipitous valleys, including the astounding Danyun Gorge, with its sheer cliffs dropping into the Fujiang River.

An extraordinary feature of Huanglong is a 2.1mi (3.5km) long gully known as the Yellow Dragon Gully where, because of a build-up of calcium deposits, limestone pools have formed. Here bacteria and algae flourish, filling the pools with a tremendous array of vibrant colors, from brilliant yellow to deep green; so vivid they recall the famous dyeing pools of North African cities such as Fez. These multi-colored, travertine pools set within a high, tranquil valley, with the snow fields looming above, create a startling, unforgettable picture. The most famous of the many hot pools is Pearl Boiling Lake, a large pool with temperatures hovering comfortably around the mid seventies fahrenheit.

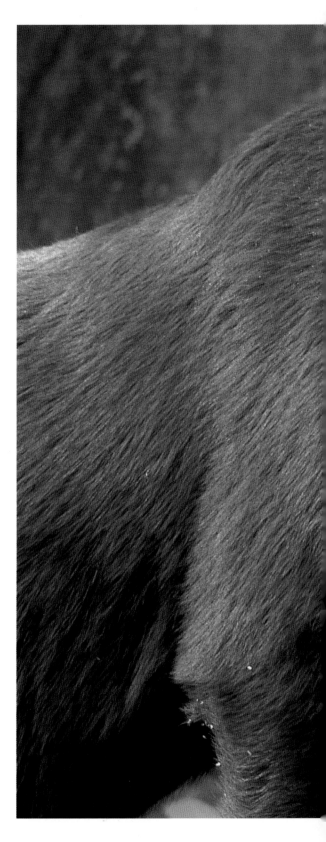

Some two-thirds of the area is forested, with local species such as Chinese hemlock, dragon spruce and maple found in the lower regions. Further up are substantial stands of larch, fir, spruce and birch. As the altitude increases, the forests eventually peter out into alpine meadows, and sparse shrub-cover. Local Tibetans use the higher pastures for seasonal grazing and even cultivate

small patches of land. Above 15,748ft (4,800m) perpetual snowfields dominate the landscape. Sixteen species of rhododendron are found in Huanglong, as well as *Fargesia denudata* and *Fargesia scabrida*is, both vital sources of food for China's giant panda.

The giant panda, one of the most endangered animals on earth, and one of the best known thanks to its being adopted by the WWF-Worldwide Fund for Nature as their official mascot, is the most important animal found here. Although panda numbers are not believed to be large, Huanglong nevertheless provides an important refuge, linking up as it does to other protected zones. This interlocking network of reserves is vital as pandas range over vast areas, as does the Sichuan golden snub-

(ABOVE) The travertine pools of Yellow Dragon Gully.

(RIGHT) The endangered Sichuan golden snub-nosed monkey.

nosed monkey, which also seeks refuge in the area. Other threatened species which have found sanctuary in this isolated setting include the leopard, the brown bear and the Asiatic black bear. Among the birds common to the region are five species of pheasant.

Because tourism has been given such high priority in recent years, the number of visitors has risen dramatically, from 50,000 annually in 1989 to 160,000 in 1991. Most visitors are Chinese, nearly all visiting Huanglong and Jiuzhaigou on the same trip. Crowding has now become a serious problem, particularly during summer and religious festivals. All the indicators point to even greater growth. The main road leading into Huanglong from Chengdu has been upgraded, reducing travelling time from twelve to ten hours. There are plans to construct an airport/heliport at Songpan. Hotel accommodation is constantly expanding as more

and more people flock to Huanglong, hoping to glimpse what is left of its isolated splendor before it vanishes, in the process hastening it on its way.

FAUNA

- Mount Huangshan shelters around 300 species of animals, over half of which are birds, including the famous oriental white stork.
- Among the larger mammals are the endangered black bear; the civet; the Chinese ferret-badger, the pangolin; the wild dog; and the elegant clouded leopard.

FACILITIES

Accommodation is often a problem, and the North Sea Hotel, located on the mountain's peak, has been known to accommodate 2,000 visitors at a time. While construction of more hotels is being undertaken, these will inevitably distract from the balanced beauty of the site while encouraging even more visitors to make the arduous journey. Access to Mount Huangshan is usually from Shanghai via Wuhu, a 12 hour journey by rail and road; by bus from Haangzhou, a journey of nine hours; or from Tunxi, which is on the railway line to Nanjing. Once at the foot of the mountain, the climb up thousands of steps to the summit takes at least six hours. There are rest and refreshment areas on the way up and 30mi (50km) of footpaths leading to the most famous lookouts and beauty points.

and it is around this period that the first wave of great pilgrimage which inspired so much artistic celebration of the mountain began. By the period of the Yuan Dynasty (1271-1368) over 60 temples had been established on the mountain. Perhaps the greatest act of devotion came in 1606, during the Ming Dynasty, when Fahai Meditation Temple and Wonshu Temple were built and connected by stairs cut into stone.

Originally on the site of the Yangste Sea, seismic activity 100 million years ago during the Mesozoic Era drove the earth's crust upwards. The multi-peaked landscape has been carved out of this uplift by the effects of erosion and glacier activity. The mountain is well known for its 'forests' of upright boulders and pillars, waterfalls, pools, lakes and hot springs, the most famous of which are located between Purple Cloud Peak and Peach Blossom Peak at 2,067ft (630m), their waters remaining a constant 107°F (42°C). Watching snow flakes melt near these springs during winter is considered one of the most soothing delights available in all of China.

Despite the seeming predominance of rocky surfaces, over half the region is in fact forested. Masson Pine is typical on the low-lying ground, while deciduous forest, such as Huangshan oak and beech emerges on higher ground, and at the top can be found alpine grassland. Several endemic plant species have been placed in jeopardy because of the great demand for them due to their ornamental or supposed medicinal value. Scattered throughout the area are individual trees that are revered for their great age - some are well over

(ABOVE) Endemic Huangshan pines set against distinctive rock features of the mountain.

(RIGHT) Typical craggy rock pillar.

1,000 years old - or else for their bizarre shapes or dangerous and unusual locations - some seemingly about to topple over cliffs or down chasms. The buffer zone surrounding the mountain consists mainly of forest or tea plantations.

Mount Huangshan shelters around 300 species of animals, over half of which are birds, including the famous oriental white stork, and 24 species of fish. Among the larger animals are the endangered black bear, the civet, the strikingly beautiful and greatly endangered clouded leopard, the Chinese ferret-badger, the pangolin, the wild dog, also threatened, and the stump-tailed macaque.

As is the case with all of the great scenic beauty sites of China, the number of tourists visiting Mount Huangshan has leapt spectacularly in the last few years, and this is despite its relative inaccessibility. In 1979 280,000 people visited the site. Ten years later that figure had doubled. This has placed enormous pressures on the site's facilities which have been limited so as not to detract

from the mountain's beauty and to avoid the aesthetic disappointment created from such large crowds, particularly in the summer and during festivals.

MOUNT TAISHAN

To walk up Mount Taishan is to make a pilgrimage: it is to share not only in a place of great beauty, but in a cultural tradition of nature worship which has existed over thousands of years. Rising suddenly out of the Shandong plain, Mount Taishan's many peaks, all of great beauty, reach to the heavens.

The Scenic Beauty and Historic Interest Zone of Mount Taishan is centered around the mountain's main peak, known as Jade Emperor peak; six brooks and numerous valleys radiate from this point. Mount Taishan is breathtaking in its wealth of natural wonders. Added to these are the many dedications left by the pilgrims who

MOUNT TAISHAN

LOCATION

Mt Taishan is located in central Shandong Province, just north of Tai'an City, N 36° 11' to 36° 31, E 116° 50' to 117° 12'.

AREA

The base of Mt Taishan covers an area of 102,000ac (42,600ha).

FEATURES

Rising suddenly out of the Shandong plain Mt Taishan reaches to the heavens. The mountain has many peaks all of great beauty and the Chinese Emperors made pilgrimages there for thousands of years.

FLORA

- The flora is diverse and known to comprise 989 species, of which 433 species are woody and the rest herbaceous.
- Medicinal plants total 462 species and include multi flower knotweed, Taishan ginseng, Chinese gromwell and sealwort.

FAUNA

- Over 200 species of animals, in addition to 122 species of birds.
- Large-scaled fish Varicorhinus macrolepis is found in running water at 1,000 to 2,600ft (300 to 800m).

(LEFT) Tiger leaping gorge.

During the Ming Dynasty (1368-1644), Azure Cloud Temple received several hundred thousand worshippers annually. Precise details about present numbers of visitors and facilities are not available, but the mountain is inundated with tourists during holiday and festival times.

journeyed to the mountain to worship Heaven and Earth. The buildings, arches, paved steps, stone tablets, inscriptions on cliff walls and bridges, as well as the more ancient temples and ruins, far from marring the beauty of Mt Taishan, add to the sublime aesthetics of the mountain's natural features.

An example of a such a human addition is the 'longevity bridge'. This bridge crosses the West Brook at the top of the 1,000ft (300m) high cliff from which the brook falls into the 'neck' of the bottle shaped, deep-bellied pool known as the Black Dragon Pool. Standing before the Black Dragon Pool you are able to take in a scene that includes a background of green hills which contrasts beautifully with the dark pool, waterfall, high cliff, and red bridge. It has not been only aesthetic sensitivity which has motivated the building on Mt Taishan - the main motivation has been spiritual. There are numerous temples including a nunnery named the Palace to the Goddess Doumu alongside the 'stepped waterfall of three pools' where the Chinese scholar tree 'Reposing Dragon' resides. Another site of interest is the South Gate to Heaven which was built at the axis of the climb to the summit above a zig-zagging path of 1,630 steps.

There are also many places where nature's beauty has been left untouched, such as the 'Peach Blossom Ravine'. Situated on the north western foot of Mt Taishan's northern slope, the ravine is 6mi (10km) in length with many peaks and cliffs along its sides. Patches of dense forest and clumps of bamboo are interspersed with pools, waterfalls and flowering fruit trees. Large-scaled fish *Varicorhinus macrolepis* is found in running water at 1,000 to 2,600ft (300 to 800m). Considered a delicacy in the Qing Dynasty, it is one of the five most famous edible fishes in China. The granite rock of the ravine is smooth surfaced and colored with yellow, red, black, white, and blue spots. In spring the whole ravine is covered in peach blossoms enchanting the senses, but at all times the ravine is a place of great beauty.

Vegetation covers 80% of the area; it is densely wooded, but information about its composition is lacking. The flora is diverse and known to comprise 989 species, of which 433 species are woody and the rest herbaceous. Medicinal plants total 462 species and include multi flower knotweed, Taishan ginseng, Chinese gromwell and sealwort, which are renowned throughout the

country. Some trees are very old and famous, notably the 'Han Dynasty Cypresses' (planted 2,100 years ago by Emperor Wu Di of the Han Dynasty), 'Tang Chinese Scholar Tree' (planted 1,300 years ago), 'Welcoming Guest Pine' (500 years old) and 'Fifth Rank Pine' (named by Emperor Qin Shi Huang of the Qin Dynasty and replanted some 250 years ago).

KEOLADEO
NATIONAL PARK

K eoladeo National Park has had a long and colorful history during its almost 150 years of existence. The terrain of 7,096ac (2,873ha) is unusual for a national park in that the landscape it comprises is entirely man-made, only coming into existence in the 1850s when a grand irrigation project was constructed in the Gangetic Plain. The project was conceived around flood waters from the Gambira and Banganga Rivers which it was hoped would flow bi-annually into this newly-created network of sluices, dykes and canals, creating a sophisticated irrigation area.

The engineers' calculations proved correct and today the system still functions, with the first inundations coming with the summer monsoons, when the region is flooded to depths of 6.5ft (2m).

A colony of open-billed storks.

LOCATION

Eastern Rajasthan, just south-east of Bharatpur and 31mi (50km) west of Agra,
N 27° 07' to 27° 12',
E 77° 29' to 77° 33'.

AREA

7,096ac (2,873ha).

FEATURES

- Keoladeo is considered one of the great bird breeding and wintering sites in the world, especially for aquatic species.
- The terrain is unusual for a national park in that it is man-made, only coming into existence in the 1850s when a grand irrigation project was constructed in the Gangetic Plain, made up of a system of sluices, dykes and canals.
- The park is subjected to flooding twice a year.

FLORA

- Much of the park is marshlands, with extensive beds of weeds, reeds and Paspalum distichum, a perennial amphibious grass.
- In the north of the park are forests, consisting mainly of Kalam, Jamun, and Babuk.

Average rainfall during this period, which lasts little more than a month, is 26in (660mm). The second flooding occurs around October when the Ajan Bund, a dam upriver, is drained for winter cultivation. After this second inundation, the national park slowly dries, so that by the beginning of the following summer, less than half of the terrain is still wetland. In the north of the park are forests, consisting mainly of kalam; jamun; and babuk; as well as some open woods and shrubland areas.

This continual process of inundation and drainage quickly created a new terrain consisting of a network of flat marshes and non-perennial marshlands, which provided ideal homes for ducks and other waterfowl. Although originally intended as both an irrigation system and a flood control device, the then owner of the land, the Maharajah of Bharatpur, being an enthusiastic shooter, quickly established the emerging marshlands as a duck hunting reserve. While this arrangement was less than perfect for the ducks, at least it ensured that the newly established flora remained protected. This in turn encouraged other animals and birds to inhabit this oasis in the middle of an area which is quite dry outside the monsoon season and which experiences blazing hot summers with temperatures approaching 122°F (50°C).

When Keoladeo finally became a bird sanctuary 100 years later, the habitat was still relatively undisturbed, and the transition to total protection took place after the last of the 'great shoots' conducted by the then Maharajah in 1964, the same year that the last leopards in Keoladeo were exterminated. The Maharajah retained his shooting rights up until 1972, and today the land is under the control of the Rajasthan State Government, and Keoladeo National Park is acknowledged as one of the most important bird breeding grounds and wintering sites in the world, particularly for aquatic species. There is an abundance of food available for the birds, including over 50 species of fish, and extensive beds of weeds and reeds and Paspalum distichum, a perennial amphibious grass.

Amongst the 364 species of bird which have been recorded in Keoladeo National Park are various types of heron, stork and cormorant, as well as shoveler, common and cotton teal, Indian shag, sandpiper, darter, white spoonbill, oriental ibis, tufted duck, combed duck and the ruff. Two of the park's most treasured birds are both cranes: the sarus crane, renowned for its magnificent courtship dance; and the endangered Siberian crane.

Unlike almost all migratory birds, the Siberian crane does not follow migration routes through instinct, but learns them by joining large flocks as a young bird and flying with them across the Himalayas to India. Conservationists, alarmed when the numbers of Siberian crane found in Keoladeo fell to single digit numbers, are now trying to introduce Siberian cranes bred in captivity to the wild Siberian cranes still flying to Keoladeo, hoping they will be accepted and taught the way back to Siberia. If they are rejected, the migratory route will be lost forever. The same dilemma is befalling Siberian cranes in Iran. Only in China are they still migrating in numbers.

Land birds include warblers, babblers, bee-eaters, bulbuls, and chats, as well as an impressive collection of birds of prey, the most spectacular being the eagles: imperial, short-toed tawny, spotted and crested serpent. The park also shelters a colony of magnificent osprey.

Water snakes and turtles thrive in the aquatic conditions, as do Indian python and green rat snake. Of course the presence of so many birds attracts a vast array of predators including the Bengal fox, the jackal, the striped hyena, the common palm and small Indian civets; the fishing cat, the leopard cat, the jungle cat, and the famous Indian grey mongoose. Also present are the rhesus macaque, blackbuck, smooth-coated otter, and Indian porcupine. There are at least 700 feral cattle within the park, which compete with the other wildlife for forage.

The question of grazing rights is a particularly thorny one in Keoladeo. Up until 1982, when it was outlawed, about 2,500 cattle and domestic water buffalo used the national park for grazing. In protest against the ban, locals tried to force their way into the park, which is surrounded by a 20mi (32km) long, 6.5ft (2m) high stone wall. Eight protesters were shot dead by police forces defending the park, and many more locals were injured, creating a climate of ill-feeling and mistrust. Ironically, it is now thought that controlled grazing is beneficial to Keoladeo, as the cattle helped clear the waterways of aquatic grass which, now unchecked, is strangling many of the water channels. The Bombay Natural History Society has taken to calling for a re-introduction of limited grazing, arguing that cattle droppings provided a vital source of nutrients.

FAUNA

- More than 360 species of bird have been recorded in Keoladeo, including open-billed stork, shoveler, common and cotton teal, Indian shag, sandpiper, darter, white-breasted kingfishers, white spoonbill, oriental ibis, tufted duck, and combed duck, ruff, short-toed eagle, sarus crane and the endangered Siberian crane.
- The many predators include the Bengal fox, the jackal, the common palm and small Indian civets, the fishing, leopard and jungle cats, and the famous Indian grey mongoose.
- The leopard, which used to roam here, was hunted into extinction.

FACILITIES

Lodging is available within the park itself at the Shanti Kutir Forest Lodge, booked through the Forest Department, and the more expensive ITDC Forest Lodge, booked through the Tourist Department. The town of Bharatpur is close to the national park. Boats are available for birdwatching. Potential visitors should check that the area is safe before leaving for Keoladeo.

(LEFT) Blackbuck.

(ABOVE) A flock of
wading painted storks.

(RIGHT) A short-toed
eagle and her chick.

MANAS
WILDLIFE SANCTUARY

Famous for its broad-banked rivers, its tranquil pools, gently undulating grasslands, forests and spectacular vistas of foothills climbing the horizon to the distant, blue-hazed peaks of the Outer Himalayas, Manas Sanctuary is the most diverse of all of India's wildlife reserves, and one of the most picturesque. Sadly it has in recent years become embroiled in ugly, local political struggles, with both park wardens and animals being killed, and protected forest attacked.

Previously known as North Kamrup, Manas Sanctuary has been under various types of preservation since the establishment of a forest reserve within the region in 1907; a process of protective upgrading which continues with the hope that it will, once its present problems are solved, be granted the status of a national park. Such a move would unite it with Bhutan's Royal Manas National Park, which it abuts. There have also been calls to

nearly triple its current size of 96,577ac (39,100ha) to 270,959ac (109,700ha). Although located in the foothills of the Outer Himalayas, Manas Sanctuary is a surprisingly low-lying area, with altitudes only ranging up to 500ft (150m). Manas Sanctuary is only a small section of the Manas Tiger Reserve, which encompasses an area of just under 617,500ac (250,000ha) in addition to the region covered by the sanctuary, forming a protective zone for a vital wildlife migratory route, ranging from West Bengal to Arunachal Pradesh and Bhutan.

Named after the Manas River, which itself was named after the Goddess Manasa, the river flows through the western section of the sanctuary, where it divides into three. Plans by Bhutan to dam the Manas and Sankosh Rivers were cancelled after protests that it would destroy the entire ecosystem of the region, as the two rivers, together with many smaller rivers, streams, and pools, carry vast

MANAS WILDLIFE SANCTUARY

LOCATION
In the districts of Barpeta and Kokrajhar, in the foothills of the Outer Himalayas, Assam, spanning the Manas River and bounded to the north by the Bhutan border,
N 26° 37' to 26° 50',
E 90° 45' to 91° 15'.

AREA
96,577ac (39,100ha).

FEATURES
- The sanctuary possesses broad-banked rivers, tranquil pools, undulating grass-lands, forests and spectacular vistas of foothills climbing to the distant peaks of the Outer Himalayas.
- It is the most diverse of all of India's wildlife reserves, and one of the most picturesque.
- Together with the Manas Tiger Reserve, the sanctuary forms a protective zone for a vital wildlife migratory route ranging from West Bengal to Bhutan.

FLORA
- In the north are dense tropical forests, and tropical rainforest and dry deciduous forests in the south and east.
- The west is dominated by open grassland, making up half of the sanctuary's area, and which includes large sections of high savanna grass.

- The sanctuary shelters 21 endangered animals including the one-horned Indian rhinoceros.
- The tiger, also greatly threatened, has its second largest population in all of India here, with 123 recorded in 1984.
- Other cats present include the fishing, marbled, and golden cats; and the graceful clouded leopard is sometimes seen.
- Among arboreal animals are many species of langur, a mischievous-looking, long-tailed monkey sometimes known as the leaf monkey, including the golden langur, a species endemic just to the sanctuary and neighboring Bhutan National Park.

FACILITIES

All foreigners must first obtain a special visitor's permit before entering Manas Sanctuary. Old-style dormitory accommodation is available inside the Manas Sanctuary at Mothanguri Bungalow, and there are camping grounds and rest houses scattered throughout the whole of the tiger reserve. Boat trips and elephant excursions are available and guides can be hired. Potential visitors should first check to see if the recent unrest has calmed down and if there are adequate numbers of park wardens on duty.

quantities of silt and rocky debris down from the foothills when they are in flood. This forms great alluvial terraces, with crevices cut by river channels slicing through them. There are also patches of swamp and sections rich in silt deposits. Although it is often flooded during the monsoon season, the sanctuary's land-based animals are never menaced by drowning as they are in other parts of India such as Kaziranga, because of easy access to higher ground.

The region's hot, sultry climate has created heavy tropical forest in the north, and tropical rainforest and dry deciduous forests in the south and east. The west is dominated by open grassland, which accounts for about a half of the sanctuary's area, and which includes wide sections of high savanna grass.

Within Manas are to be found some of India's most magnificent animals, 21 of which are endangered, including the Indian rhinoceros, which numbered 75 in 1980. Most famous of all is the tiger, which has its second largest population in all of the sub-continent here: 123 in 1984. Other cats include fishing cat, marbled cat, and golden cat, leopard, and the graceful clouded leopard, also endangered. Among the arboreal animals are many species of langur - a mischievous-looking, long-tailed monkey, sometimes also called the leaf monkey - including the golden langur, a species endemic just to the sanctuary and neighboring Bhutan National Park. Its breeding grounds have been disrupted by the establishment of Amtika Village which, although located in the sanctuary's buffer zone, is in an area favored by golden langur.

A pair of greater adjutant storks.

(RIGHT) A young male tiger, one of Manas' most threatened species.

There has been fairly extensive penetration of the reserve's buffer zone by locals, with 144 villages housing 55,000 people, mainly agriculturalists, many of whom slash and burn areas to create space for crops, and occasionally poach. The traumatic effects the behaviour of the locals has had on the wildlife is vividly demonstrated by the extraordinary clashes between farmers and elephants witnessed here in recent years.

The Indian elephants, which number about 3,000 and are used to roaming throughout the whole of the tiger reserve as well as Bhutan National Park, often enrage the farmers by trampling their crops. Sometimes the elephants, along with hog deer, actually make raids on the crops, seeing them as a convenient source of food. The farmers retaliate by attacking the elephants, usually with spears, sometimes aflame. This only provokes the elephants into charging their tormentors. Fatalities have been known to occur.

The sanctuary's extensive water system is home to the last pure strain stock of water buffalo in India, and also attracts over 300 species of birds, including the endangered Bengal florican, which numbered only 34 in 1984. Other birds common to the sanctuary include various types of hornbill; spot-billed pelican, and both lesser and greater adjutant stork, while snakes include the vine snake, flying snake and the Assam trinket snake.

NANDA DEVI
NATIONAL PARK

NANDA DEVI NATIONAL PARK

LOCATION

In Chamoli District, within the Garhwal Himalaya, and comprising the catchment area of the Rishi Ganga, N 30° 16' to 30° 32', E 79° 44' to 80° 02'.

AREA

155,692ac (63,033ha).

FEATURES

- All of the basin is above 11,483ft (3,500m). It is encircled by high mountain ridges on all sides except the west, where an inaccessible gorge drops to 6,890ft (2,100m).
- The Upper Rishi Valley is known as the 'Inner Sanctuary'.
- The highest peak is Nanda Devi West, at 25,646ft (7,817m), the eighth highest in the world.

FLORA

- Fir, birch and rhododendron are all common.
- Alpine meadows, mosses and lichens are present in the upper ground, and scrub juniper is common inside the 'Inner Sanctuary'.

One of the most spectacular national parks on earth, Nanda Devi is today closed to almost all visitors. Only a handful of professional mountaineers with international credentials are now permitted to venture into a basin known as the 'Inner Sanctuary'. The closure, which took effect in 1983, was a drastic action which sadly needed to be taken. Although only opened to tourists in 1949, Nanda Devi National Park suffered a rapid and brutal decline due to the carelessness of those who visited, leaving vast amounts of litter at base camps and on trekking routes. Logging too has played a decisive role in degrading the environment, stripping the landscape of cover, leading to rock slides, avalanches and erosion. The trees were cut mainly to provide fuel for the expeditions. Erosion was also exacerbated by the introduction into the region of goats and sheep by porters. The more trekkers came, the more porters were required and the more fuel was required. So the provincial government of Utter Pradesh was forced into taking the extreme step of denying the beauty of Nanda Devi to visitors today in the hopes of trying to preserve it for tomorrow.

There are some sites which hold a particular magic for those initiated into a special part of its history, and in Nanda Devi's case the initiated are the world's professional mountaineers. The mountain is the stuff of legend, and the accounts of the many attempts to scale it - the successes and disasters - hold a unique place in alpine lore. Yet those who do not follow mountaineering with such passion are still moved by Nanda Devi; not by its history, but by the beauty of the site itself: its majestic peaks and solemn slopes inspiring that unaccountable awe felt whenever encountering anything which is breathtakingly beautiful yet by its nature unobtainable.

This distant, elusive glory is acknowledged in the origins of its name: Devi is the title of a mother goddess who took many forms, including Annapurna. In the instance of Nanda Devi, she is believed to be the manifestation of Parvati, the consort of Shiva. Thus the mountain's name

sanctifies its natural beauty and acknowledges its spiritual dimensions. The mountain has been revered by Hindus as a sacred place for centuries, and every 12 years a solemn procession winds its way up to the foot of Trisul mountain (23,360ft - 7,120m) to worship the 'Blessed Goddess'.

The park is a large glacial basin which has been deified as the 'Sacred Basin', and is encircled by high mountain ridges on all sides except the west, where a deep, inaccessible gorge plunges down to 6,890ft (2,100m). Except for this gorge, all of the basin is above 11,483ft (3,500m). An upper valley, Rishi, is known as the 'Inner Sanctuary'. The highest peak is Nanda Devi West, at 25,646ft (7,817m), the eighth highest mountain in the world. There are 12 peaks over 21,000ft (6,400m) including Dunagiri at 23,182ft (7,066m); Changbang at 22,520ft (6,864m); and Nanda Devi East at 24,390ft (7,434m).

• As many as 118 species of birds have been recorded in Sagarmatha National Park, including many songbirds, doves, pigeons and species of duck, as well as the impeyan pheasant, the national bird of Nepal.
• Perhaps the most dazzling creatures in the park are its butterflies, ranging from the rare silver hairstreak and the endemic orange and silver mountain hopper through to the fragile snow apollo, which lives at extremely high altitudes.

FACILITIES

There is an airstrip at Lukla, south of the park boundary, which has a regular air service from Kathmandu. Everest View Hotel and associated Shyangboche airstrip above Namche Bazar are the most sophisticated tourist facilities but they do not account for a high proportion of visitor use. A national park lodge has been built at Tengpoche providing sleeping accommodation, with detached cooking and toilet facilities, as well as basic food and drinks. Other accommodation is available in 'sherpa hotels' and some villagers take in guests. An imposing visitor center, providing information and interpretative services, has been constructed on the hill adjoining Namche Bazar.

recorded in Sagarmatha National Park, many using the Dudh Kosi valley as a migratory route. They include many songbirds, doves, pigeons and species of duck, as well as the impeyan pheasant, the national bird of Nepal. The high mountains and crags are the domain of raptors such as the Himalayan griffon vulture and the lammergeyer, which live up to 25,000ft (7,600m), while the yellow billed chough has been sighted up to 27,000ft (8,200m), nearly as high as Sagarmatha herself.

Perhaps the most dazzling creatures in the park are its butterflies, ranging from the rare silver hairstreak and the endemic orange and silver mountain hopper through to the fragile snow apollo, which lives at extremely high altitudes.

The beauty and grandeur of Sagarmatha National Park attracts tourists from all parts of the globe. The number of annual visitors has increased from 20 in 1964 to about 4,000 by the mid 1970's. Ironically, those who come in search of its remote and natural beauty are in danger of destroying the very thing they seek. The sherpa way of life is also under threat, and it is imperative to find a way of keeping the delicate balance of nature and co-existence so that all may benefit.

The Sherpa village of
Namche Bazar, last
stop on the way to Mt
Everest base camp.

SINHARAJA FOREST

SINHARAJA FOREST

LOCATION

Situated in the south-west lowland wet zone of Sri Lanka, within Sabaragamuwa and Southern provinces, N 06° 21' to 06° 26', E 80° 21' to 80° 34'.

AREA

21,300ac (8,864ha).

FLORA

- Most of the forest's plants are unique; there are also many plants which are used for medicinal purposes.

FAUNA

- Numerous birds inhabit the forest including azure flycatcher, green tree warbler, crimson-backed woodpecker, emerald-collared parakeet and white-breasted kingfisher.
- Toque monkeys and purple-faced leaf-monkeys spend much of their time in the treetops.
- Some of the larger animals which inhabit the floor of the forest are pig, sambhur, mouse deer and civet cats.

(ABOVE) Pitcher plant growing on the rainforest floor.

The legendary Sinharaja forest covers 21,300ac (8,864ha) of steep and rugged country in the south-west lowlands of Sri Lanka. It is the island's only sizeable remnant of undisturbed rainforest, a mere fragment of the immense slab of thick jungle which once covered the entire south-west of the country.

The protected area of the forest covers a hilly area, where the tallest peak is about 3,860ft (1,170m). There are several valleys and ridges which run parallel from east to west, curving to the north-west and which are dissected by cross valleys. The forest has a dense canopy about 132ft (40m) high, which encloses a dark and humid environment. All of the trees have grown straight and tall in their struggle for the light. At ground level vegetation is sparse; the nutrient poor red-yellow soil is covered with leaf litter and decomposing branches. The earth is moist and despite being shallow has a great capacity for holding water and releasing it slowly - the area receives a rainfall of over 98in (2,500mm) per year. The roots of the trees are shallow, relying on the protection of the other trees and the forest as a whole to keep them standing. Tree ferns and staghorns are found throughout the forest as are ground and tree orchids. Climbing cane palms wind themselves up the tree trunks, also joining in the struggle for sunlight.

There are many cool fresh streams which run through the park, protected by the forest from the harsh glare which leads to dry creek beds and drought in the cleared areas around the forest. Along these streams grows soft foliage, ferns and some flowers including the scarlet flowered wild cardamom. The streams are full of fresh water crabs and sweet prawns, and leopards often come to the streams not only to drink but to feed as well. Also found in the streams are spiny cat fish, spike-tailed paradise fish and titteya fish.

Numerous birds inhabit the forest including azure flycatcher, green tree warbler, crimson-backed woodpecker, emerald-collared parakeet and white-breasted kingfisher. Most of the bird life in

the rainforest is in the canopy and cannot be seen from the forest floor, but they also frequent waterways and pools. Toque monkeys and purple-faced leaf-monkeys also spend much of their time in the treetops. Some of the larger animals which inhabit the floor of the forest are pig, sambhur, mouse deer and civet cats.

The people of the Sinharaja area harvest cane from the rainforest as well as the sweet juice of the wild kitul palms, resin, wild cardamom and reeds. There are also many plants in the forest which are used for medicinal purposes. Most of the forest's plants are unique, as is the forest itself. It is thought that the Sinharaja forest is a relic of Gondwanaland. After surviving relatively intact after Sri Lanka broke off from India to form an island, this small pocket of contiguous virgin rainforest is all that remains of the original environment.

Up until recently, this remnent jewel has survived relatively unscathed, but that situation is changing rapidly as human encroachment threatens the forest's delicate balance. Owing to its inaccessibility and steep, hilly terrain, the reserve remained untouched until 1968 when a government directive was issued to extract timber for the plywood sawmill and chipwood complex established at Kosgama. From 1971 until 1977, when logging was banned, about 3,700ac (1,400ha) of forest in the

LOCATION

On the south-eastern coast of Queensland, S 24° 35' to 26° 23', E 152° 30' to 153° 30'.

AREA

Approximately 3,360sqmi (8,600sqkm).

FEATURES

- Fraser Island is the largest sand island on earth - it is 76mi (122km) long, 3 to 15mi (5 to 25km) wide and reaches 775ft (235m) in height. The sand extends 1,000 to 2,000ft (30 to 60m) below the present sea level. The dunes of this region are the oldest (between 10,000 and 140,000 years old) and highest (apart from Mt. Tempest on nearby Moreton Island) of all known sand dunes.

FLORA

- The rainforest canopy includes rare kauri pines and satinays, brush box and hoop pine, soaring 200ft (60m overhead).
- Apart from the rainforest, there are areas of sclerophyll forest, woodland, grassland and heath. Some of the sclero-phyll forests are very tall, being dominated by large eucalypt species such as blackbutt, tallowood, brushbox and scribbly gum, while other forests are dominated by much lower eucalypts and banksias.

FRASER ISLAND

Take a walk through what is left of Fraser Island's rainforest and you will be amazed and saddened. The canopy of rare kauri pines and satinays, brush box and hoop pine, soars 200ft (60m) overhead, while down on the ground palms, mosses and enormous ferns thrive next to crystal clear waters. The sheer beauty of the surroundings transports you back to a time when the earth was more in balance and its creatures lived with a harmony that ensured longevity. But then you keep walking, and you are saddened, perhaps even angered, at what you see. For much of the forest

has been logged. Rare species have been ripped out of their delicate habitats to be turned into highly prized timber. The fragile ecosystems of these forests have been built up over thousands of years, only to be destroyed overnight by shortsighted greed. How important it is then, that Fraser Island should now be protected and recognized by World Heritage listing.

This World Heritage site encompasses all of Fraser Island and it constitutes one of the world's greatest coastal sand masses. Fraser Island itself is the largest sand island on earth. It is 76mi (122km)

(FAR LEFT) Synchronized humpback whales.

(ABOVE) One of Fraser Island's unique dingos atop a sand dune.

(LEFT) Loggerhead turtle hatchlings making their way to sea.

FAUNA

- The dingoes on Fraser Island are of particular interest, as they are considered to be one of the purest strains in the country.
- The birdlife is very rich, with over 230 species known to inhabit the area including cockatoo, peregrine falcon and sea eagles.
- Marine life is also abundant, with large populations of various fish species, crabs and prawns. Larger sealife is particularly rich - substantial numbers of dugongs and dolphins are found, but the waters are most famous for the large number of humpback whales that stop here to rest on route south to Antarctica

FACILITIES

Fraser Island is currently estimated to receive around 200,000 visitors a year, this number having increased rapidly since 1975. Facilities for visitors include several resorts and further accommodation for 10,000 campers in developed camp sites. Up to 5,000 additional campers may utilize beach areas, fishing camps and other sites at peak times. Access is via vehicular barges at Rainbow Beach in the south, or River Heads, near Hervey Bay, where there is also a fast catamaran service. Air Charters are available from Hervey Bay and Eurong on the island.

long, 3 to 15mi (5 to 25km) wide and reaches 775ft (235m) in height. The sand extends down to 200ft (60m) below the present sea level. The dunes of this region are the oldest (between 10,000 and 140,000 years old) and highest (apart from Mt. Tempest on nearby Moreton Island) of all known sand dunes.

The great marvel of Fraser Island is that it is made entirely of sand. It's something that you find you have to keep remembering. Especially when walking through the magnificent forests - these ancient giants are growing in sand. And there is another great surprise: the system of freshwater lakes which are perched up high on the sand dunes. Found in the south of the island, these lakes are made possible in the sandy environment by a lining of organic material which prevents the water from percolating away. Lake McKenzie is one of the most beautiful, with its crystal clear water and pure white sand bottom, it exhibits an alluring shade of turquoise that is absolutely stunning.

There is a remarkable diversity of vegetation to be found in the area. Apart from the rainforest, there are areas of sclerophyll forest, woodland, grassland and heath. Some of the sclerophyll forests are very tall, being dominated by large eucalypt species such as blackbutt, tallowood, brushbox and scribbly gum, while other forests are dominated by much lower eucalypts and banksias.

The dingoes on Fraser Island are of particular interest, as they are considered to be one of the purest strains in the country. The birdlife is very rich, with over 230 species known to inhabit the area, including some very large and spectacular species such as the glossy black cockatoo, peregrine falcon and sea eagles. Marine life is also abundant, with large populations of various fish species, crabs and prawns. Larger sealife is also found, including substantial numbers of dugongs and dolphins, but the waters are most famous for the large number of humpback whales that stop here to rest on route south to Antarctica. Small pods of humpbacks typically rest for two to five days in the sheltered waters between Fraser Island and the mainland before recommencing their migration south from their northern wintering grounds.

It is unfortunate that this area of outstanding beauty has been a center of heated environmental debate in the past, particularly with regard to logging and sandmining. Mining ceased in 1976 and rehabilitation was undertaken in the areas

mined. In the 1970s this activity affected, 840ac (350ha) but the Queensland government has negotiated the surrender of all remaining mining leases and lease applications, and no further sand mining will take place. Mined land on Inskip Peninsula, in linear strips affecting almost, 480ac (200ha) has been revegetated, but does not represent a re-establishment of the original ecosystems. The topography of the 360ac (150ha) of mined dunes of Fraser Island has been irreversibly simplified by mining and the original forest has been removed.

The forests of Fraser Island, Cooloola and the Kin Kin areas have been subject to logging for around 130 years. The mainland rainforests were largely cleared for timber and then agriculture, but the forests of the sandmassses have fared considerably better. Many of the largest and oldest trees were removed, and the resource of scrub timber declined to unsustainable levels in some instances after less than 30 years of logging. Although there is no evidence that any species have been eliminated from the region due to logging, the forest structure, floristic composition and relative species abundance have been altered. Agreement was reached between the Queensland government and the timber industry to cease all logging on Fraser Island by 31 December 1991. World Heritage listing will hopefully draw people's attention to the importance of this area and lead to an understanding of how crucial it is that its integrity be maintained.

Lake Mckenzie.

LOCATION

Off the east coast of
Queensland,
S 24° 30' to 10° 41',
E 142° 30' to 150°.

AREA

83,688,000ac
(34,870,000ha).

FEATURES

- The Great Barrier
Reef is the world's
largest expanse of
living coral reefs.
Stretching about
1,250mi (2,000km)
along the eastern
coast of Queensland,
this giant maze of
coral reefs comprises
some 2,500
individual reefs inter-
spersed with 71 coral
islands called cays.

FAUNA

- This is an area of
tremendous scientific
importance, hosting
many unique forms of
marine life, including
over 1,500 species of
fish, more than 400
species of coral and
4,000 of molluscs, as
well as numerous
species of sponges,
crustaceans,
anemones, marine
worms, and
echinoderms.
- Pelagic (open ocean)
fish species such as
marlin and mackerel
move through the reef
regularly, while
demersal (bottom
living fish) live in and
around the reefs.

(ABOVE) Birth of a sea
star.

(RIGHT) A giant
wrasse.

AUSTRALIA

GREAT BARRIER REEF

Coral reefs are to the ocean what rainforest are to the land: both are enormous storehouses of biodiversity. The Great Barrier Reef is the world's largest expanse of living coral reefs. It is an area of tremendous scientific importance, hosting many unique forms of marine life, including over 1,500 species of fish, more than 400 species of coral and 4,000 of molluscs, numerous species of sponges, crustaceans, anemones, marine worms, and echino-derms.

Stretching about 1,250mi (2,000km) along the tropical eastern coast of Queensland, this giant maze of coral reefs comprises some 2,500 individual reefs interspersed with 71 coral islands called cays. Some of the reefs are separated by channels as narrow as 660ft (200m), while some are up to 12.5mi (20km) apart. Most are submerged, but many are exposed at low tide. These reefs are composed of calcium carbonate: the result of the ability of certain plants and animals - in particular the corals - to produce substantial skeletons of this material.

The reef's physical characteristics show major variations with latitude, allowing it to be easily classified into three sections:

- the sector north of 16°S mainly encom-passes shallow waters less than 120ft (36m) above the continental shelf. At the edge of the shelf is a line of wall reefs and between that line and the mainland are numerous patch reefs. A feature of this sector are the many low wooded islands (cays) which support important mangrove habitats;
- the central sector between 16°S and 21°S has a greater water depth up to 400ft (55m) and is characterized by scattered platform reefs several miles apart. There is a channel up to 30mi (50km) wide separating these reefs from the mainland;
- the sector south of 21°S is the deepest part of the reef up to 480ft (145m). It is charac-terized in the north by a series of tightly packed reefs separated by narrow channels carrying strong tidal currents, and in the south by some large patch reefs with vegetated cays.

These substantial variations in habitat have

There are also many smaller, often brightly colored fishes, such as butterfly fish, which live in very restricted and strongly defended territories.

- Other marine fauna include six species of turtles - notably the loggerhead and green turtles, which have important breeding sites located on the reef area. Whales, dolphins, and dugong are prolific and are all protected.
- The cays and islands support 242 species of birds, including 40 species of sea birds, 21 of which have breeding colonies in the area. Of the 240 land bird species, 109 have breeding sites recorded.

FACILITIES

Visitors to the Great Barrier Reef spend over 2.2 million visitor days a year on the reefs and islands. Resort guests make extensive use of reefs and waters for recreational activities, including fishing, diving and snorkelling, water sports, sightseeing and reef-walking. Tourism is allowed to occur under permit within all except preservation and scientific research zones, that is in 99.8% of the marine park. Whilst the area designated free from tourism or fishing may seem low, it must be recognized that the marine park encompasses large areas of open water, so that the proportion of reef so designated is, in practical terms, much higher.

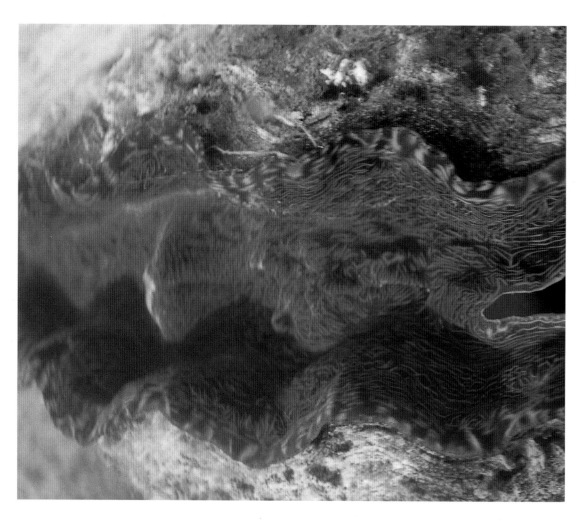

These substantial variations in habitat have allowed for an equally substantial diversity in the fauna found on the reef. In fact, the Great Barrier Reef is probably the richest marine habitat to be found anywhere. There are approximately 1,500 species of fishes, exhibiting a great variety of size, shape, color and behavior. Pelagic (open ocean) species such as marlin and mackerel move through the reef regularly, while demersal (bottom living) species such as coral trout, sweetlip, red emperor, snapper and cod spend most of their lives in and around the reefs. There are also many smaller, often brightly colored fishes, such as butterfly fish, which live in very restricted and strongly defended territories.

Other marine fauna include six species of turtles - notably the loggerhead and green turtles, which have important breeding sites located on the reef area. Whales, dolphins, and dugong are prolific and are all protected. The cays and islands support 242 species of birds, including 40 species of sea birds, 21 of which have breeding colonies in the area. Of the 240 land bird species, 109 have breeding sites recorded.

As would be expected in managing such an enormous marine park, there are numerous matters for concern. Run-off from islands and the mainland contains suspended solids, herbicides, pesticides, nutrients, and other materials which may have an effect on the reef, but the degree of threat is not certain. Prevention of unacceptable ecological impact is paramount in the Great Barrier Reef Authority's management of tourism development. The type of impact which may be associated with reef-based tourism operations include: discharge of waste, litter and fuel, physical damage to reefs from anchors, snorkelling, diving and reef walking, disturbance of fauna (especially seabirds), over-fishing or shell collecting. Oil exploration permits are in force over most of the reef between Cairns and Rockhampton, although it is government policy to prohibit all oil drilling which might damage the reef. Crown-of-thorns starfish *Acanthaster planci* have caused considerable mortality amongst corals, particularly in the central section of the reef.

With the inscribing of the Great Barrier Reef onto the World Heritage List, Australia has been charged with the responsibility to protect one of the most complex, diverse and important natural

LORD HOWE
ISLAND GROUP

LORD HOWE ISLAND GROUP

LOCATION

About 435mi (700km) north-east of Sydney, New South Wales; S 31° 30' to 31° 50', E 159° to 159° 17'.

AREA

Approximately 2,820ac (1,176ha).

FEATURES

The peaks of Mt. Gower (2,890ft - 875m) and Mt. Lidgbird (2,565ft - 777m) rise dramatically in the south and dominate the view from anywhere on the island.

FLORA

- Many of the plant species are very rare and there is a high incidence of endemism. Both mountains have sufficient altitude to have allowed the development of true mist forests on their peaks. Here we find palms, orchids, mosses, and ferns intermingled with the endemic banyan, a sub species of the Moreton Bay fig.
- Due to their successful adaptation worldwide as indoor plants, two endemic palm species are particularly renowned - the thatch palm and the Kentia palm (now officially known as Howea).

Imagine a small subtropical island covered with luxuriant growth, tall twin peaks reaching up through low heavy clouds, the shimmering Pacific Ocean lapping its shores, its forests teaming with rare wildlife, an untouched coral reef at its shores. Then you have imagined Lord Howe Island, one of the smaller natural World Heritage sites, and one of the most beautiful.

Lord Howe Island itself covers 3,500ac (1,455ha), while the tiny islets which surround it make up a further 200ac (85ha). Of the islets, Ball's Pyramid is the most striking. This is the world's highest rock pinnacle; its sheer rocky face juts dramatically up from the ocean floor, the weathered remains of an ancient volcanic island. In fact, the entire group is a remnant of a shield volcano that built up more than 4,400ft (1,400m) from the sea floor about eight million years ago.

Without a doubt it is the island's topography that makes it so spectacular. The peaks of Mount Gower (2,890ft - 875m) and Mount Lidgbird (2,565ft - 777m) rise dramatically in the south and dominate the view from anywhere on the island. On the northern side of these peaks, sheer cliffs fall hundreds of yards down to the sea. In marked contrast is the low lying sandy center of the island, which is embraced by a reef-enclosed lagoon on its western side. The Northern Hills rise gently in the north west and complete the crescent shape of the island.

This intense diversity in topography has led to the development of a wide array of flora on the island. Many of the plant species are very rare and there is a high incidence of endemism. Both mountains have sufficient altitude to have allowed the development of true mist forests on their peaks. Here we find palms, orchids, mosses, and ferns intermingled with the endemic banyan, a sub species of the Moreton Bay fig. Due to their successful adaptation worldwide as indoor plants, two endemic palm species are particularly renowned - the thatch palm and the Kentia palm (now officially known as Howea). The rainforest on the highland contrasts sharply with the patches of short grassland and dry forest on the central lowland. In the lower-lying areas, destruction of native vegetation has been virtually complete where clearings have been made for settlement, grazing and agriculture, and regrowth tends to be of invading weed species, including introduced plants such as guava, bitou bush, ferny asparagus and asparagus fern. However, adequate samples of intact lowland vegetation remain in less accessible parts of the island, some of them in special flora reserves.

Of the fauna on the island, it is perhaps the birdlife that is most notable. Around 120 different species of bird are supported in this tiny area. Sadly, nine of the fifteen species of land birds

- Twenty two native mammals are found in the park including dingo, red kangaroo, common wallaroo, marsupial mole, spinifex hopping mouse, several bat species including Australian false vampire, bilby, short-nosed echidna, several small marsupials including dunnarts and native rodents.
- More than 150 bird species have been recorded in the park, of which 66 are considered resident. These include parrots, wrens, thornbills and raptors such as peregrine falcon.
- All five Australian reptile families are represented and species include monitor lizard, thorny devil lizard, western brown snake, Ramsay's python and numerous others.

FACILITIES

Most visitors come during the cooler May to September period, with 86% of visitors arriving by road and the remainder by air. Tracks, paths and some sealed roads provide access to the monoliths and other sites within the park. Accommodation is available at Yulara tourist resort north of the park boundary. Interpretation programs are centered on the park entry station and include official guided tours and other services. The most popular activities are sightseeing, walking, climbing Uluru, scenic flights, sunset and sunrise viewing, driving, picnicking and photography.

(ABOVE) Black footed rock wallabies.

(RIGHT) Hairy footed dunnart, one of Uluru's unusual and endangered marsupials.

As with most of the Australian sites, there is a deep running interconnection between the natural and the cultural aspects of this place. It is impossible to separate the beauty and significance of the natural setting from their cultural context, and indeed the futility of attempts to define such a separation are well demonstrated here.

In its harsh and arid environment Uluru is rarely touched by rainbows.

TASMANIAN WILDERNESS

TASMANIAN WILDERNESS

LOCATION

Central and southwestern regions of Tasmania; E 145° 25' to 146° 55', S 41° 35' to 43° 40'.

AREA

3,360,000ac (1,400,000ha).

FEATURES

This enormous site protects around 20% of Tasmania's land mass.

FLORA

- Temperate rainforest covers about 30% of the area below the treeline. The tree species are Gondwanan, dominant being myrtle beech, leatherwood and sassafras.
- Huon pine, one of the longest lived species in Australia (some individuals are more than 2,000 years old) and one that has been unmercifully logged, is often found in riverine habitats.
- There are many areas of pristine eucalypt forest, with some extremely tall species, such as the mountain ash - at 295ft (90m) the world's tallest flowering plant.

FAUNA

- Two main groups of fauna may be distinguished, one contains the species such as the

The name of this site is of utmost importance, for much of the area is 'wilderness' in the truest sense. There are very few places on the globe outside of the Arctic Circle and Antarctica that are as untouched. Here it is possible to walk for days and days on end without seeing another human face, and it is just possible, if you venture long enough and hard enough, that you will come to a place where no one has walked before. The country is that wild. It is old and rugged. Glaciers have given the mountains hard faces. Rapid cool streams race underfoot. Misty cloud forests harbor secret ferns and mosses. Frigid lakes nestle high in precious hollows. Tall and ancient forests stand out in the soaking rain, defying the cold winds that blow off the desolate ridges beyond.

It is an enormous site (it protects around 20% of Tasmania's land mass), a conglomerate of numerous national parks and reserves totalling approximately 3,360,000ac (1,400,000ha). Both the rugged topography and the cool, wet climate of Tasmania are unusual in Australia. As a consequence, the vegetation has as much in common with that of South America and New Zealand as it does with that of mainland Australia, a fact verified by the numerous relict Gondwanan flora species that are to be found.

The sheer size and diversity of the area has resulted in an enormous wealth of habitats; this wilderness may truly be described as a wonderland of unusual, rare, endangered and relict species.

Temperate rainforest covers about 30% of the area below the treeline. The tree species are Gondwanan, dominant being myrtle beech, leatherwood and sassafras. Huon pine, one of the longest lived species in Australia (some individuals are more than 2,000 years old) and one that has been unmercifully logged, is often found in riverine habitats. There are many areas of pristine eucalypt forest, with some extremely tall species, such as the mountain ash - at 295ft (90m) the world's tallest flowering plant.

Two main groups of fauna may be distinguished, one contains the species such as the

marsupials and the burrowing crayfish that are relicts of Gondwanaland, the other includes rodents and bats, species that invaded from Asia after the break up of Gondwanaland. There are 37 species of mammals, six of which are endemic to Tasmania, including the well known Tasmanian devil - the world's largest surviving carnivorous marsupial (assuming that the Tasmanian tiger is extinct, a point that is actively disputed by some). Over 150 bird species are present, 13 of which are endemic, including one of Australia's rarest birds - the orange-bellied parrot. There are also 14 species of reptiles (six endemic), six frogs (two endemic) and 21 fish (eight endemic).

There is plentiful evidence that parts of this great wilderness was populated up to 30,000 years ago. Kutikina Cave, in the Franklin River Valley was the first aboriginal site where Ice Age occupation was recognized. After excavating less than one cubic yard of cave floor, more than 40,000 stone artefacts and 77lb (35kg) of bone fragments were uncovered, making this cave one of the richest prehistoric sites in Australia. Judd's

Hakore waterfall.

SHIRAKAMI-SANCHI
(SHIRAKAMI MOUNTAINS)

LOCATION

In the north of Honshu, 9mi (15km) inland from the Sea of Japan, N 40° 22' to 40° 32', E 140° 02' to 140° 12'.

AREA

24,000ac (10,139ha).

FEATURES

- This site represents the last remaining area of virgin Siebold's beech forest.
- It is the largest remaining virgin beech forest in the East Asian region.

FLORA

- The vegetation is dominated by Siebold's beech.
- Many of the 500 odd plant species found within the area are typical of Japanese flora.

FAUNA

- All the mammal species found on Honshu, with the exception of two, are found within this park.
- The Japanese black bear is common.
- There have been 87 species of bird identified within the area.
- Over 2,212 species of insect have been recorded.

FACILITIES

There are no roads, paths or man-made structures within the park. Approximately 3,000 people climb Mount Huatsumori each year.

The Shirakami mountains are home to 57,600ac (24,000ha) of pristine Siebold's Beech forest. This forest is one of Japan's predominant forest types and once covered the whole of the cool temperate zone of northern Japan. While we have sadly lost most of this forest cover to logging and other human interference, the forest of these mountains remain as the last beech forest wilderness in Japan and the largest remaining in the East Asia region.

This park is all national forest and is located entirely within the Shirakami Mountains which extend over 178sqmi (450sqkm). Almost no logging has been carried out due to its remoteness and ruggedness. These are rugged, steep sided mountains, with summits lying at altitudes up to 4,000ft (1,200m). More than half of the area comprises deep valleys with steep slopes at gradients of more than 86°F (30°C). Many streams have their sources within the area and it is an important water catchment area. The climate is cool and moist and there is heavy snow during winter.

The vegetation is dominated by Siebold's beech (Fagus crenata). This is the typical Japanese temperate forest. Many of the 500 odd plant species found within the area are also typical of Japanese flora. Not quite so typical of this forest are the large stands of dwarf bamboo which are found here, a species usually considered to be typical of warmer subtropical forests. There are several species which are endemic to the area and also many globally threatened species including numerous orchids.

All the mammal species found on Honshu, with the exception of two, are found within this park. The Japanese black bear is commonly seen in spring searching for food after a long winter's hibernation. This forest is also the northern-most habitat for primates in the world - the snow monkey, or Japanese macaque is often seen roaming the forests. There have been 87 species of bird identified within the area, including one pair of Golden eagle which is designated a National

Monument and a Special Bird due to its limited breeding record and endangered status in Japan. There are also three pairs of black woodpecker and one pair of Hodgson's hawk, similarly designated as Special Birds. There is a particularly rich population of insects, with over 2,212 species having been recorded.

There are many problems confronting the park management, including the protection of the Japanese black bear - many individuals migrate outside the park boundaries and get trapped or shot in the surrounding orchards. Another area of concern lies with the number of low flying military aircraft which often buzz the park. A project to build a logging road through the forest was halted after a nation wide protest, and thousands of people signed a petition against it. Finally the Forestry Agency gave up their plans for the road and instead established the park as a Forest Ecosystem Reserve. This protection has since been twice strengthened: firstly when it was declared as a National Conservation Area by the Environment Agency in 1992, and finally, the ultimate recognition of the park's importance, not only to Japan, but to the world as a whole, when Shirakami-sanchi was included on the World Heritage list in 1994.

coconut groves exist in the park. The marine flora is much more varied, with extensive seagrass beds in the shallower parts of the reefs and lagoons and 45 different species of macroalgae.

At least 46 different species of birds have been observed in the park, including brown boobies, red-footed boobies, common noddy, sooty tern and crested tern. Marine turtles nest on some of the beaches, including hawksbill turtle and green turtle. There is a very rich fish population, with 379 species having been recorded. Black-tip shark and white-tip shark, manta rays and eagle rays are common. Several different clam species occur, including crocus clam, giant clam, scaly clam and horse's hoof clam.

Tubbataha has remained in a relatively pristine state due to its isolation and difficult

Brown and blue footed boobies.

access. There have, however been several disturbances from activities such as blast fishing, large scale collection of sea bird and marine turtle eggs, unsustainable gathering of clams and other marine species, spear fishing, collection of fish for the aquarium trade and other disturbances to wildlife. There was a commercial operation for harvesting seaweed which employed up to 24,000 people in the area. This was halted after six months of illegal operation. There are no permanent inhabitants within the park, although some fishermen establish temporary settlements during the fishing season.

FACILITIES

Tubbataha is one of the most popular scuba destinations in the world. It is visited by more than 1,500 divers annually. Tourism generates more than US $1,000,000 annually. Two coast guard staffers and a lighthouse keeper are occasionally stationed on South Islet. There is a regular boat patrol of the park by the Tubbataha Foundation.

THUNG YAI - HUAI KHA KHAENG
WILDLIFE SANCTUARY

THUNG YAI -
HUAI KHA
KHAENG
WILDLIFE
SANCTUARY

LOCATION

Situated in Kanchanaburi and Tak provinces alongside the western international border with Burma and located at the southern end of the Dawna Range,
N 14° 55' to 15° 45',
E 98° 28' to 99° 05'.

AREA

1,493,300ac (622,200ha).

FLORA

- The principal vegetation types, is as follows: hill evergreen forest, dry evergreen forest, mixed deciduous forest, dry dipterocarp forest, savanna forest, grassland and some areas of swidden agriculture.
- The highest ground is generally covered with hill evergreen forest, also known as tropical lower montane rainforest, but slopes above 2,000ft (600m) generally support dry evergreen forest.
- At lower altitudes mixed deciduous and bamboo forests predominate.
- In particularly moist areas along rivers and streams, evergreen gallery forest is present.

(RIGHT)
Curcuma plant.

At the heart of Thung Yai Wildlife Sanctuary there is a large grassland plain surrounded by a savanna forest of cycads and phoenix palms. The plain and forest are unusual natural features and the plain gives the sanctuary its name, 'Thung Yai' meaning 'big field'. The size of this field and the uniqueness of the savanna forest are significant to the importance of the sanctuary. Not only does Thung Yai - Huai Kha Khaeng possess unique and diverse biological and geographic features but it is uniquely able, because of its overall size as well as the size of this central plain, to support large numbers of fauna.

Thung Yai and Huai Kha Khaeng are contiguous wildlife sanctuaries near Thailand's Burmese border. Across this beautiful country there are many hills, with permanent and seasonal streams forming valleys that are interspersed throughout the small lowland plains. There are many small lakes, ponds and swampy areas, both seasonal and perennial, with their own particular habitats. The watershed of the Huai Kha Khaeng, and much of that of the Huai Thap Salao rivers, are within Huai Kha Khaeng, providing homes for otters and white-winged wood duck.

Thung Yai - Huai Kha Khaeng is buffered to the north and the south by protected forests of substantial sizes. It was hoped at the time of Thung Yai - Huai Kha Khaeng's inclusion in the World Heritage list that the adjacent area in Burma would also eventually be protected, particularly as some of the animals in the sanctuary habitually travel through the forest overlapping the two countries. However this has not eventuated and the governments of Burma and Thailand have made little effort to protect this forest, seeming more interested in the trade in timber.

The sanctuary has five distinct types of forest; ranging from evergreen on the highest slopes, through dry semi-evergreen, to mixed deciduous and bamboo, dry dipterocarp, and in moist areas evergreen gallery forests. This often results in a patchy mosaic of vegetation throughout the park.

The diversity of vegetation types in the sanctuary is not merely as a result of variation in altitude and humidity; nor is it merely because of the area's status as one of the only evergreen forest refuges during the driest periods of the Pleistocene glaciations: the main reason is that the Thung Yai - Huai Kha Khaeng Wildlife Sanctuary is situated on the meeting place of four of Asia's principal biogeographic zones - the Sino-Himalayan, Sundaic, Indo-Burmese and Indo- Chinese. The resultant immense variation of species is also to be found in the fauna of the park. There are, for example, 22 species of woodpecker in the area.

The size of the wildlife sanctuary (1,493,300ac - 622,200ha) is most important as it makes it possible for viable populations of these many different species to sustain themselves. It is possibly the only place remaining which is capable of supporting a self-sustaining population of the Asian elephant. Also important are other large herbivores such as the three species of wild bovids and the largest herd of gaur in Thailand. The

FAUNA

- Thung Yai is big enough to support several of the larger and increasingly rare mammal species, such as tiger, leopard, clouded leopard, elephant, tapir, Sumatran rhinoceros, gaur, serow and hog deer. A herd of 50 gaur was seen in 1985, making it the largest herd recorded in Thailand.
- Notable bird species include white-winged wood duck, Kalij pheasant, Burmese peafowl and green peafowl.
- The park includes some 120 mammals, 400 birds, 96 reptiles, 43 amphibians and 113 freshwater fish as confirmed occurrences, with a number of species suspected as being present but not confirmed.

FACILITIES

The sanctuary is not open to the general public, but permission may be given to researchers, naturalists and education groups for specific purposes. Some 400 to 500 visitors come each dry season. Permits can be obtained from the Wildlife Conservation Division in Bangkok, or from the Chief of the sanctuary. Thung Yai is accessible by road (mostly unsurfaced) from Bangkok via Kanchanaburi. The journey takes 10 to 12 hours.

(ABOVE) Asian elephant and her calf.

necessary populations for a healthy gene pool are able to live in the sanctuary supported by the flora and, in the case of the 27 or so carnivores including tigers, by the other fauna.

Unfortunately, this is one of the features of the park which remains under threat from the proposed Nam Choan Dam project. Although the project has been shelved, there remains the possibility that it could be revived at some point in the future There was fierce opposition to the project from wildlife conservationists for two main reasons. First, the dam's reservoir would have split the sanctuary into three smaller areas, which would greatly reduce the long-term survival prospects of the larger mammals. Secondly, the reservoir would have flooded lowland habitat below 1260ft (380m). Lowland forests are already rare in Thailand; lowland riverine habitat is especially rare. Several threatened species occur almost exclusively in this kind of habitat, for example short-clawed otter, smooth-coated otter, green peafowl, lesser fish eagle, white-winged wood duck and red-headed vulture, as well as many plant species. Valley bottom habitats, such as the Mae Chan Valley

which would be flooded, are thought to provide optimal habitats for most of the large herbivores, for example tapir, elephant and wild cattle species.

An interesting geographical feature in the sanctuary is the presence of limestone sink holes. Many are only about 33ft (10m) in length with a diameter of 66ft (20m), but some are more than several miles long and 830ft (250m) wide, with a depth of up to 100ft (30m). These large caverns are worthy of exploration. As well as the limestone sink holes there are numerous mineral licks throughout the park, which are frequented by animals.

Thung Yai - Huai Kha Khaeng has also been under threat from poaching, logging and agricultural development. Poaching is the most persistent problem and more resources are badly needed to effectively protect the area Despite being the largest conservation area in Thailand, Thung Yai receives roughly the same allocation of manpower and money as sanctuaries half its size. It is to be hoped that its placement on the World Heritage List will assist in the protection of this magnificent and very special place.

the north of the delta, where the branch river Chilia forms the border with the Ukraine, the area is slowly sinking.

Throughout the reserve are lakes covered with flooded reed beds, islets, flooded willows, riverine forests of willow and poplar, cane fields, sand and mud beaches, wet and dry meadows, steep banks, sand and rock areas, and forests. Despite a low rainfall (450mm - 18in pa) the area is very humid. Floating and fixed islands of reedbeds covering a total area of 390sqmi (1,000sqkm) are dominated by the species *Phragmites australis..* Blooms of water lilies are scattered throughout the marshes, but in recent times threatening blooms of algae have also spread over the water surface.

The wetland area is a special place for many rare and endangered birds. Species include cormorant, pygmy cormorant (2,500 pairs comprising 61% of the world's population), white pelican, Dalmatian pelican (perhaps now only 25 to 40 pairs, on the floating islands on lake Hrecisca, which represents 5% of the world population), night heron, Sqacco heron, great white heron, little egret, purple heron, glossy ibis, white stork, mute swan, white tailed eagle, marsh harrier, osprey, Saker falcon, red-footed falcon, sandwich tern, as well as common, whiskered and black tern. White-headed duck and the slender billed curlew have been seen on rare occasions.

The delta holds huge numbers of anatidae in the winter with counts of 500,000 white-fronted goose, up to 500 lesser white-fronted goose, 45,000 red-breasted goose (a globally threatened species with almost 95% of the world wintering population present here), 150,000 teal, 14,000 pintail, 40,000 shoveler, 32,400 red-crested pochard, 970,000 pochard, 13,000 ferruginous duck, and 1,500 red-breasted merganser. Also inhabiting the floating islands are otter, European mink and wild cat.

Sadly the delta ecosystem though 'intact' has been seriously degraded. Activities within the delta area, as well as development and land use outside of Romania in the lower Danube and river basin, have caused major damage to the delta. The flood basin of the lower Danube has been largely 'reclaimed' from the river and is now used for agriculture. Agriculture and irrigation flood the river with chemicals - pesticides, herbicides and fertilizers, and the river is heavily polluted by nitrogen, potassium and chlorine. Salinity levels have also risen due to the extensive use of the river's fresh water for irrigation. The removal of approximately four-fifths of the reed beds in the lower Danube has further contributed to pollution as the beds had previously acted as a natural filter system. Deposition of silt has drastically changed and some areas have been made drier due to increased drainage. In the Delta area itself the construction of canals - cutting off the river's natural meandering course to make the water flow more direct, land reclamation and irrigation have greatly changed the delta environment. Over-fishing, the introduction of Chinese carp and the reshaping of parts of the lake system to create breeding ponds which are for the most part ineffective have adversely affected the native fish species - especially the wild carp, and this in turn affects the bird life of the delta.

Some of these problems are within the power of the Romanian Government to fix, but what the condition of this delta makes us most aware of is the need for European co-operation on environmental issues. If Europe is to maintain its water ways in any semblance of health - and in fact what is needed is improvement not maintenance - then it must work as one body: co-operation is vital if we are to have a healthy future.

FAUNA

- Over 300 species of bird have been recorded, of which over 176 species breed, the most important being: cormorant, pygmy cormorant, white pelican, Dalmatian pelican, night heron, squacco heron, great white heron, little egret, purple heron, glossy ibis, white stork, mute swan, white-tailed eagle, marsh harrier, osprey, Saker falcon, red-footed falcon, sandwich tern, common tern, whiskered tern, and black tern.
- The delta is very important for fish with 45 fresh water species present including threatened representatives of the acipensenidae.
- Otter, wild cat and European mink are to be found on the floating islands.

FACILITIES

Under the previous regime, parts of the delta were heavily used for tourism, with up to 100,000 visitors annually, mostly concentrated at two hotels along the Sulina channel, although many people camped along major channels in the summer. Permission is needed to visit the nature reserves which are closed during the bird breeding season. The areas away from the three main channels are rarely frequented.

(ABOVE) A purple heron catches a fish.

SKOCJAN CAVES

SKOCJAN CAVES

LOCATION

In the commune of Sezana in the Socialist Republic of Slovenia, 8mi (13km) east of Trieste, N 45° 40', E 14° 02'.

AREA

440ac (200ha).

FEATURES

- This collection of caves, grottos and galleries, underground canyons and rivers, is one of the most beautiful speleological sites in the world, a remarkably well-preserved example of subterranean karst formation.

- A system of underground passages have been created by the Reka, which enters Skocjan grotto via one of these subterranean passages 1,200ft (350m) long. The flow rate through this sunken passage, which is one of the largest subterranean canyons on earth, can be as high as 11,000 cubic feet (300 cubic meters) a second.

FLORA

- The Sokolak, Globacak, Sapen dol and Lisicina chasms have similar vegetation and, due to the microclimatic conditions present in the collapsed galleries and the shallow chasms of the river valley, a mixture of habitats are represented corresponding to the floras of central Europe, the

This collection of caves, grottos and galleries, underground canyons and rivers, is one of the most beautiful speleological sites in the world, a remarkably well-preserved example of subterranean karst formation.

Devoid of any but the most essential structures, such as bridges and safety walkways, visitors entering Skocjan Caves find a strange, cool world of glistening limestone faintly yet atmospherically lit. Weird shadows are cast from stalactites formed on irregular ceilings, and unexpected chasms constantly unsettle and fascinate the visitor. The curious, disorientating sights are matched by the unique aural experience of the caves: the persistent drip of water falling into pools, the consoling rush of the waterfalls, the visitor's own echoing footsteps resounding strangely; as though someone were following. This otherworldly aspect is perhaps why Skocjan, unlike similar nearby cave systems, such as Postojna (where a train rushes tourists past turnstiles and through underground caverns with fanciful names such as 'Paradise Grotto'), has fortunately escaped the crasser elements of modern mass tourism. Even though, before the wars in the former Yugoslavia began in 1991, more than 50,000 people visited the caves each year, the experience was always a personal - almost introspective - one, as though the dark dignity and somber beauty of the caves demanded respect.

The site covers an area of 40ac (200ha), and includes four deep chasms: Lisicina and Sapen Dol to the north, Globocak to the west and Sokolak to the south; while in the east is the Reka River, which begins as a shallow canyon. A system of underground passages have been created by the Reka, which enters Skocjan grotto via one of these subterranean passages 1,200ft (350m) long. The river, after being glimpsed at the bottom of two deep chasms, disappears into another passage 1.3mi (2km) long. The flow rate through this sunken passage, which is one of the largest subterranean canyons on earth, can be as high as 11,000 cubic feet (300 cubic meters) a second. The caves' many underground passages lead eventually to the Gulf of Trieste, a distance of around 8mi (13km). The total length of the cave system is over 3mi (5km), and the maximum depth reached is around 760ft (230m). The Mahorcic grotto has several underground lakes as well as five cascades. Other important sites within the system include the Okroglica Chasm, and the Great Valley and Little Valley. Altogether there are 25 waterfalls, including one with a leap of more than 530ft (160m).

Although today the caves are home to just five species of bat, there were small human communities living inside them during the Middle Stone Age, and the archeological remains of five prehistoric cemeteries have been discovered. During the Iron Age a fort was erected, which in turn was built over by the Romans. A fortified village was established nearby sometime during the Middle Ages, and today there are three interesting villages within the World Heritage site, with a total population of about 65 people, all of whom recognize the importance of preserving the Skocjan Caves.

This, unhappily, has become more difficult in recent times. Despite the exceptional level of preservation of the caves themselves, and such precautions as locking them at night, the cave system has been threatened by water pollution, which reached high levels in the Reka River in the 1970's and 1980's. Much of this was caused by dumpings by a fibreboard factory. The intro-

Mediterranean, Submediterranean, Illyrian and Alpine all of which are present side by side in the Great Valley. This unique combination allows Mediterranean species to grow next to alpine species.

FAUNA

• The system of grottos has typical speleo-fauna including habitat for Microtus nivalis and the endemic Proteas anguinus..

• The underground galleries hold five species of wintering bat in reasonable numbers.

FACILITIES

Being so close to Trieste in Italy, the Skocjan Caves are easily visited in a day trip from that country. They are also close to Ljubljana, where there are various types of accommodation including hotels, hostels and a camp ground, and where buses run to the caves during the months they are open to the public, from the beginning of June until the end of September. The caves are also not far from the beautiful site of Lake Bled, where hotels and inns can be found. Before attempting to go to the caves, any prospective visitor should first ensure that the political situation permits safe passage.

duction of a biological treatment plant as well as strict curbs on dumping and the purchase of cleaning equipment were all expected to drastically reduce pollution. But when in 1991, the nearby Slovenian capital of Ljubljana became the first city to be subjected to aerial bombardment in Europe since 1945, a new menace to the caves

arose. Although the Serbs have, for the time being at least, brought a halt to their war with Slovenia, it is impossible to predict what effects, if any, the wars in the former Yugoslavia, and war-related economic difficulties, will have on what A C Waltham, in his book 'The World Of Caves', called 'one of the wonders of the world'.

GARAJONAY
NATIONAL PARK

GARAJONAY NATIONAL PARK

LOCATION

In the central portion of la Gomera, Canary Islands, north of and between Tajaque to the east and Chipude to the west, N 28° 05' to 28° 12', W 17° 10' to 17° 18'.

AREA

9,560ac (3,984ha) - just over 10% of the island surface.

FEATURES

- Naturalists believe that Garajonay's botanical diversity closely resembles that which existed in the Miocene and Pliocene Epochs; that is, one to twenty-five million years ago. Thus it can be seen as a living relic from the Tertiary Period, an example of subtropical vegetation which gradually disappeared everywhere else in Europe as the continent's climate grew colder.

FLORA

- 70% of the park is woodland.
- To the west of the park is heathland, where heather, bog myrtle, lichens and mosses grow.
- There are 450 flora species, 34 found only on La Gomera, and eight endemic to the park itself.

This national park of 9,560ac (3,984ha) is located near the center of the island of La Gomera, one of the seven isles which comprises the Canary archipelago in the Atlantic Ocean, off the north-west coast of Africa. It was on this island that Columbus last stopped before sailing for the 'New World' in 1492. And here, in 1488, that the 'Guanches', an indigenous group of unknown origin, were massacred by the Spaniard, Pedro de Vera, only five years after he 'claimed' the Canary Islands in the name of Spain.

Garajonay National Park occupies a striking situation atop an eroded central plateau with steep escarpments that fall in steps of hundreds of feet. The altitude of the park ranges from up to 4,900ft (1,487m). Unlike the other islands in the group, La Gomera, which possesses the classic volcanic island silhouette when seen from out at sea, hasn't experienced any volcanic eruptions in recent times and so has kept its forests, which have flourished in the mature soil and the subtropical climate. Scattered about are upright boulders of volcanic origin known as 'roques', which stand like lonely sentinels, reminiscent, in the distance, of the statues of Easter Island.

The park is made up of what used to be six forests, which were confiscated from the aristocracy and turned over to local governments in 1812. Scattered within these former municipal holdings are small pockets of land which are, even today, still privately owned. These dense forests play a vital role in the life of the island, helping mist to condense, thus augmenting the island's water supply, which is also maintained by streams and underground springs.

Although the park has been designated 'public property' for well over a century, that didn't stop intensive logging which between 1879 and 1964 saw the island's total forested area decrease by sixty-five percent. Given the importance of the forests to the island, it is amazing to think that laws had to be passed in 1964 to restrict logging. It is a classic example of how a local population, which was fully aware of the importance of the forests,

still persisted in putting short-term profits derived from logging ahead of the long-term benefits of maintaining an important source of drinking water. In 1970, a law was introduced to help restore the forests.

Because of the changes in altitude, there are many different types of vegetation, the most important being the lush stands of laurel forest.

The predominance of laurel accounts for the park's two most famous bird species, the white-tailed laurel pigeon and the dark-tailed laurel pigeon. Other tree species including palo blanco; and til, or sesame.

Although seventy percent of the park is woodland, the landscape is dominated by dramatic volcanic outcrops and a series of deep ravines known as 'barrancos'. To the west of the park is heath land, where heather, bog myrtle, lichens and mosses grow. Altogether there are 450 flora species, 34 found only on La Gomera, and eight endemic to the park itself. Such a remarkable profusion of plants over a relatively small area is all the more important because naturalists believe that Garajonay's botanical diversity closely resembles

Agando rock - one of Garajonay's many rugged features.

(RIGHT) Around 70% of Garajonay is woodland.

that which existed in the Miocene and Pliocene Epochs; that is, one to twenty-five million years ago. Thus it can be seen as a living relic from the Tertiary Period, an example of subtropical vegetation which gradually disappeared everywhere else in Europe as the continent's climate grew colder.

Spain's past management of its many magnificent natural sites has often been faulted. The debasement of the Spanish Mediterranean coastline in the name of package tourism is one of the great conservation and aesthetic disasters of post-war Europe. And the degradation of Las Marismas, once an extensive marshlands of great importance to migratory birds, now largely given over to tourist development and the cultivation of early spring crops, such as strawberries and asparagus, is particularly disturbing. Aware of these past failures,

Spanish authorities seem this time to be committed to preserving what remains of Garajonay's forests.

Until recently, grazing still occurred on the outskirts of the park and fires, perhaps deliberately started, are still a menace. As a response to these problems, the park's management have created both floral and entomological inventories and instituted a genetic rescue plan for those endemic species most at risk. They have also divided Garajonay into zones, including a highly restricted biogenetic reserve zone. It is hoped that by these means, Garajonay will be able to preserve what is left of its forests.

GÖREME
NATIONAL PARK AND THE ROCK SITES OF
CAPPODOCIA

The environment of Göreme Valley, situated in the Iranian-Anatolian desert, is both bleak and fantastic. The valley is visually dominated by 'Akdag', a peak of 4,370ft (1,325m) which has been created by deep rifts within the earth's crust. But it is the regular conical shapes, and the 'fairy chimney's' with their slabs of rock balanced delicately on top, the pillars, columns, obelisks and needles sometimes reaching a height of 130ft (40m), that are most astounding. There are also stunning irregular formations. The valley, once a plateau, is now an erosion basin. The area was volcanically active for a long time. In the late Pliocene period volcanic eruptions vomited large quantities of ash into the atmosphere, covering an area of 3,900sqmi (10,000sqkm). Lavas which poured over the plateau between the late Pliocene

and early Pleistocene periods have been heavily eroded, leaving remarkable formations. The harder stone is often white but sometimes orange and showing layers of different colors in horizontal stripes, both contrast strongly against the sparse green vegetation and the blue sky. One of the most unusual geological landscapes on earth, the valley is like an open air gallery with so many of these spectacular formations in such a small space.

The Göreme Valley has been under continuous human occupation for at least 16 centuries. As a result of this the fauna and flora of the area have been greatly modified. The flora found in the valley is mostly agricultural; vineyards and orchards of apples, pears and quinces. Some tiny pockets of native flora and fauna remain, but their existence has been sadly neglected. Crop

GÖREME
NATIONAL PARK
AND THE ROCK
SITES OF
CAPPODOCIA

LOCATION

In Nevsehir Province of Central Anatolia, between Nevsehir city and the towns of Avanos and Urgüp, N 38° 26', E 34° 54'.

AREA

23,000ac (9,576ha).

FEATURES

The valley is visually dominated by 'Akdag', a peak of 4,370ft (1,325m) which has been created by deep rifts within the earth's crust.

(ABOVE) The desolate wasteland of Göreme Valley.

213
Europe

- It is the regular conical shapes, and the 'fairy chimney's' with their slabs of rock balanced delicately on top, the pillars, columns, obelisks and needles sometimes reaching a height of 130ft (40m), that are most astounding.

CULTURAL

- The Göreme Valley has been under continuous human occupation for at least 16 centuries. Here, from the 4th through the 13th century AD, a relatively harmonious human-dominated landscape has developed, which is integrated into and makes use of the spectacular natural setting.
- The 'fairy chimneys' and exposed cliff faces have been part excavated and tunnelled so as to form churches, and various rock-cut chambers. These caves served as refuges, residences, storage and places of worship. There are also other classified monuments found within the valley but outside the limits of the park.

(RIGHT) Some of the rock-cut chambers found in Göreme Valley.

cultivation is a main source of income for the people of the area, as are the rearing of livestock and market gardening - beans, chick peas, lentils, garlic. The population of the Göreme Valley is predominately agrarian with some crafts such as onyx ceramic, pottery, and weaving of rugs and carpets. In the 1980's tourism became a major economic resource. Conservation of the park depends upon the continuance of the traditional rural lifestyle of its inhabitants. Land management, farming and building is closely monitored by the Turkish government and regulated by laws. The protection of the park is executed in two zones, the first of which includes the main sites and two villages and is entirely protected from the destructive aspects of human change.

The changes which the human inhabitants have wrought on the natural rock formations, over the centuries are far more pleasing than those wrought on the flora and fauna of the region. Cones, pillars, and exposed cliff faces have been excavated since the 4th century BC. The excavations include residences, refuges, storage rooms, and places of worship. The seven churches within the valley date from the 10th to the 13th centuries. They contain the most magnificent frescoes, the images in which are historically significant because many monks retreated to Cappodocia as a result of the iconoclast push within the church which attempted to restrict religious artistic portrayal to certain forms. The area was also a place of refuge in the time of the Moslem invasion of Turkey. The religious images are from a range of time periods and styles, from geometrical patterns to scenes from the life of Christ. It was not only the availability of material which prompted the hollowing of stone, but also the need for a refuge, a place to escape persecution, a place to hide both themselves and their religion. The inhabitants have however become predominately secular over time, as Christianity ceased to be a reason for hiding many Christians moved away and those who still make their homes in the rock do not do so out of fear.

The natural forces which created the rock formations of Cappodocia now threaten their continued existence. There are still occasional earthquakes in the Cappodocia area, and erosion and water damage are a constant problem. Murals are painstakingly and faithfully restored but collapsing walls and rockfalls pose serious problems. Tourism also threatens to damage the soft stone formations and the art of the rock-hewn churches, not only through inadvertent erosional damage but also through deliberate vandalism. Although it may be possible to protect the park from human change, it cannot be protected from nature and time.

FACILITIES

The main center for visiting the national park is at the town of Göreme where there are a diversity of facilities including interpretative trails, hotels and camping accommodation, information services, restaurants, cafes, shops and transport to the various cultural remains scattered around the park. There is an open air museum only a few miles from Göreme, which encloses many of the historical church structures dating from Byzantine times.

(ABOVE)
The weathered landscape of Cappodocia.

215
Europe

HIERAPOLIS-PAMUKKALE

Hierapolis - Pamukkale National Park is home to one of Europe's most spectacular natural formations. A series of hot thermal springs bubble up from the rock and overflow down the mountainside through a succession of terraced pools. The semi-circular travertine pools, like hewn steps, delicately meander down the upper third of the slope, ranging in height up to 20ft (6m). The pools extend over 1.5mi (2.5km) and some are as wide as 1,650ft (500m). Waterfalls tumble down over the steps of the terraces. The water from these springs is heavily laden with calcium carbonate, and over the centuries this has caused white stalactite formations to form over the rims of the basins, suggesting a fanciful picture of dazzling white icy pools melting in the hot and humid Mediterranean summer. In winter, the snow on the slopes, and the 'icy' hot pools transform the cliffs into a fantastic spectacle, like a fairy winter palace.

These remarkable pools are situated on the northern side of the Curuksu River Valley. Above the Curuksu plain, the travertine cliffs extend

FACILITIES

Seasonal volunteer working parties are housed in the restored cottages. Access by visitors is restricted by lack of communication and landings (between May-June) are controlled by the warden. Several independent charter companies also run shorter trips but visitors remain on board at night.

(ABOVE) Puffins.

guillemots, razorbills and kittiwakes. It was once the sole British home of the fulmar, and there are over 30,000 pairs nesting on the islands. The most populous of the feathered inhabitants is the enchanting puffin, with approximately 300,000 breeding pairs. Manx shearwater and the storm petrel are also common, and the area is one of the few nesting sites in Europe of the Leach's petrel. The grassy heaths of Hirta house a colony of great skua, and golden plover and whimbrel visit the area, as well as greylag geese and barnacle geese.

The islands' isolation gave rise to a distinct sub-species of wren, the St Kilda wren, and amongst its mammalian population there is a type of wood-mouse found only within the archipelago. The feral Soay sheep have been the subject of much scientific study, and may descend from primitive sheep introduced to Britain in about 5,000BC, or may have come over with the Vikings in the 9th and 10th century.

Botanically, the most striking environmental features of the archipelago are the high humidity, reflected in the peaty soils and prevalence of humidity-seeking oceanic plants such as the liverwort, and the effects of salt spray. The presence of salt-resistant plants hundreds of yards above sea-level indicates the spray-drenching that must occur during storms, and much of the grassland has a sub-maritime character. The huge numbers of sea birds create excellent fertilizer in certain areas, with pasture supporting a good stock of Soay sheep on Hirta and Soay, and Blackface sheep on Boreray. Hirta is the only island with any area free enough from the effects of salt water to allow the growth of substantial non-maritime plant communities.

Seven acres (three hectares) of land are occupied by the Ministry of Defence for use as a missile radar tracking station. This has a local effect as have small peat cuttings, and areas of derelict turf cutting and derelict cultivation. It would seem that the only likely threats are from the possibility of accidental oil spills (this is a particularly busy part of the Atlantic Ocean), which would affect the feeding stations of St. Kilda's vast seabird populations, and from proposals which have been made to construct additional military radar facilities.

Much literature has been produced about the mystical archipelago of St. Kilda, and its history has ensured it a continued place in our global consciousness. The fact that a community which survived physical hardships and isolation for over 2,000 years should be destroyed by our modern ways is a tragedy that is of some value only if we learn from it, and act to prevent similar situations from occurring in the future.

The Oceans: Our Lifeblood Threatened

The predominant physical feature of our planet is the oceans. They cover two-thirds of its surface. They play a key part in the chemistry of the atmosphere, hydrological cycle and in determining climate and weather conditions.

Life in the oceans is dominated by physical factors such as waves, tides, currents, salinity, temperature, pressure and light intensity. These contribute to determining the makeup of the biological communities which in turn have an effect on the composition and chemistry of the oceans.

The vastness of the oceans has led people to believe that they cannot be harmed. This is not so. Before this century the notion was largely correct because fewer people were exploiting the resources of the sea and they were limited by the very simple technologies at their disposal. During this century, however, the number of people exploiting ocean resources has increased dramatically and extensive developments have been made in ocean technologies. Not only have older, simpler methods been improved, totally new techniques have also been discovered which make new uses possible. These include radar and sonar that have contributed to safer navigation and easier detection of fish; man made structures on the continental shelf which make possible the routine exploration and exploitation of petroleum far from land; freezer-factory trawlers capable of spending long periods at sea not only catching fish but processing them on board to a market ready state; and design and material improvements in shipbuilding.

These technological advances have led to dramatic increases in our capability and effort to harvest fish stocks, but we have probably approached the limit. During the 1980s the world marine fish catch increased steadily, reaching 84 million tonnes a year in 1988. Many fisheries scientists consider the limit of fisheries production to be around 100 million tonnes per year. With the possible exception of deep ocean squid and Antarctic krill, new resources will not be readily available to exploit. At present the technology to exploit squid is limited and many believe krill could not sustain extended heavy fishing pressure. If these assumptions are valid then by the year 2000 it is estimated that the demand for fish and shellfish would exceed supply by around 20 million tonnes. This would raise world market prices and increase the pressure for governments to sell marine products to derive development income. Such a situation could become critical for many tropical developing countries that derive between 40 and 100% of their animal protein from fisheries.

The interface between the land and sea, the coastal zone, consists of continental shelves and coastal plains. This area is not simply a transition area but has special characteristics of its own. It is a band of highly diverse ecosystems and habitats that are among the most biologically productive on earth. These include extensive intertidal mudflats, rocky shores, sandy beaches, mangroves, saltmarshes, estuaries and other wetlands, seagrass and

by war and sanctions - becomes more desperate than it already is.

Incredibly, the greatest threat of all to Durmitor is a local, man-made one. Just 20mi (32km) upstream from Tara's canyon is a lead processing factory which for years stored its waste waters, rich in deadly mercury, in a series of storage tanks which are now full, and which cannot be replaced. Rather than have 2,000 workers lose their jobs, the government decided to allow the waste waters to be discharged into the Tara. The ecological effects of this on such a pristine environment would be almost too tragic to contemplate. The immediate result would be to ensure that the Tara would become biologically dead. In the face of international protest, the dumping has not gone ahead. Whether the decision not to dump is permanent or not, nobody knows, especially since sanctions imposed by resolutions of the United Nations Security Council now preclude inspection of the site.

A plan to dam Tara's canyon so as to produce hydro-electricity was initially cancelled in the face of international pressure, but has since been given the go-ahead in the belief that it will have 'minimal impacts on the conservation of the area'.

So it is with trepidation that Durmitor faces the future, in the face of these serious and menacing threats.

FACILITIES

Facilities for visitors were more than adequate before the Yugoslavian Wars erupted. There were hotels and camp sites available inside and near the park, as well as picnic sites and hiking routes. It was possible to take three and four-day rafting trips down the Tara, or overnight horseback excursions into the mountains. Travel to Montenegro should not be undertaken until sanctions and the wars have ended.

(ABOVE) European brown bear.

(LEFT) Male chamois.

THE AMERICAS

NORTH AMERICA
Canada • Mexico • USA

CENTRAL AND SOUTH AMERICA
Argentina • Brazil • Costa Rica • Ecuador
Guatemala • Honduras • Panama • Peru

KLUANE WRANGELL - ST. ELIAS AND GLACIER BAY
NATIONAL PARKS

LOCATION

In the southeast corner of Yukon Territory, spanning the boundary with Alaska, N 60° 00' to 61° 20', W 137° 00' to 141° 00'.

AREA

39,336,000ac (16,390,000ha).

FEATURES

• The majestic glaciers and snow covered peaks of four mountain ranges dominate the landscape of this, the largest protected area on earth.

• Mount Logan and majestic Mount St. Elias, at 19,600ft (5,950m) and 18,100ft (5,490m) respectively, are two of the three highest mountains in North America.

FLORA

• The coastal forest is in evidence up to about 3,300ft (1000m) above sea level. Forests of blue-green Sitka spruce and hemlock spruce grow along the Bremner River and in the narrow canyons below the mountains.

• Up to 3,600ft (1,100m) there is a wide cover of montane forest, dominated by white and black spruce.

(PREVIOUS PAGE)
Young grizzly bears in Kluane National Park.

The majestic glaciers and snow covered peaks of four mountain ranges dominate the landscape of this, the largest protected area on earth. Here, in a site listed jointly with Canada and the United States, towers the mighty Mount Logan and majestic Mount St. Elias. These peaks, at 19,600ft (5,950m) and 18,100ft (5,490m) respectively, are two of the three highest mountains in North America.

The four dominating mountains chains in this area are St. Elias, Wrangell, Kluane and Chugach Mountain Ranges. Together, they act as a trap for the moist Pacific weather fronts, resulting in the spectacular glaciers and snowfields for which the area is renowned. The parks central plateau is the largest non-polar icefield in the world, and incorporates the Bagley Icefield and the dazzling Seward Glacier. There are more than 100 named glaciers, with an equal number as yet unnamed. Two of the world's most sizeable glaciers, the Hubbard and the Nabesna, are found here, as well as the famous Malaspina Glacier. All the glaciers are remarkable for their beauty and variety, with some advancing, some retreating, and others which appear stable. The greatest array of surging glaciers on earth are present here.

The region is a source of continual fascination, as the landscape of the park is constantly being modified by glacial activity. Examples of moraines (rocky debris deposited by glacial activity) can be found adjacent to the Kluane, Bernard and Russel Glaciers, with other distinctive glacial features such as kames, kettles, cirques and eskers spread throughout the adjoining areas. The bedrock of the park spans the three major eras of the earth's geological history, the Paleozoic, Mesozoic and Cenozoic. Metamorphic rocks such as marbles, slates and schists are present in the parks, as well as sedimentary rocks derived from volcanic activity during the Cenozoic Era, and

A bank vole.

granites from Cretaceous times. Also manifest are layers of volcanic ash, originating from the Nataghat Mountain and glacier area, which were deposited as recently as 1200 years ago.

There are four extensive ecological communities supported within the parklands. These are: coastal forest, montane forest, the subalpine zone and the alpine tundra. Coastal forest is in evidence up to about 3,300ft (1,000m) above sea level. Forests of blue-green Sitka spruce and hemlock spruce grow along the Bremner River and in the narrow canyons below the mountains. Up to 3,600ft (1,100m) there is a wide cover of montane forest, dominated by white and black spruce, as well as balsam poplar, trembling aspen and grey leaf willow, buffaloberry, scrub birch, hypnum moss and red bearberry; while muskeg and bog plants are found in the marshy areas. At higher

(ABOVE) Gray wolf.

largest underground river systems in North America. The water from this lake surfaces in springs in the floor of the Maligne Canyon 10mi (16km) down the valley. Other lakes of unsurpassed beauty include Lake Louise, Peyto Lake and Emerald Lake. There are also many breath-taking waterfalls, including Takakkaw Falls and Twin Falls in Yoho.

Vegetation in the four parks strongly reflects climatic conditions, the three major eco-regions are montane, subalpine and alpine, with montane found in the lowest areas. Characteristic of montane is lodgepole pine, white spruce and Douglas fir, but there are less common areas of montane vegetation in the extensive wetlands of Vermilion Lake and in the sand dunes near the Athabasca River. The subalpine region supports Engelmann spruce, subalpine fir and some lodgepole pine on the lower slopes, while in the upper subalpine area the greater snowfalls and shorter growing seasons give rise to open forests of stunted trees (krummholz). The harsh alpine eco-region is devoid of trees. There are alpine meadow areas, but a large part of this region is rock, glacier or permanent snowfields.

The smallest animal in the parklands is the tiny pigmy mouse, while the grizzly bear is perhaps the most impressive and well known, although

- The montane areas support lodgepole pine, white spruce and Douglas fir.
- The subalpine region supports Engelmann spruce, subalpine fir and some lodgepole pine.
- The harsh alpine eco-region is devoid of trees. There are alpine meadow areas, but a large part of this region is rock, glacier or permanent snowfields.

FAUNA

- The smallest animal living in the parklands is the tiny pigmy mouse, while the grizzly bear is perhaps the most impressive.
- The parks protect at least two endangered species, the bighorn sheep and the gray wolf, and other mammals include black bear, moose, wapiti, mule deer and mountain goat.
- Over 280 species of birds have been identified within the parks, although most visit only during the summer months.
- Two of the birds of prey that find protection here are the golden eagle and the bald eagle, which have seriously declined in numbers across the continent.

FACILITIES

Yoho: With approximately 1.1 million visitors per year, this park has five campgrounds, three for tents and recreational vehicles; two for tents; also one group tenting area and one winter camping area. There are three roadside

commercial accommo-
dation facilities totalling
152 units and two
backcountry lodges.
Visitor services are
available at Field, British
Columbia. Banff:
Approximately 8 million
people pass through the
park each year. About
3.3 million stop to use the
park. There is one town
(Banff) and one visitor
center (Lake Louise) with
a total capacity of about
8,000 overnight visitors
and almost 2,500
campsites within the park,
and 1,000mi (1,575km)
of hiking trails. Kootenay:
2.5 million visitors
annually.
Accommodation is in 403
campsites in three
front-country
campgrounds, one
100-group tenting area
and five bungalow
camps. Jasper: More
than 2 million visitors
annually. The park
contains 1,752 campsites
(of varying standards) in
12 front-country
campgrounds and 200
sites reserved for group
tenting. In addition, there
are over 100 designated
back-country campsites.
There is accommodation
for about 4,500 visitors
in the town of Jasper,
and a well-developed
network of marked hiking
trails and cross-country
skiing routes (some
600mi - 1,000km).
Permits must be obtained
for overnight stays along
trails. There are infor-
mation centers in Jasper
town and the Columbian
Icefield.

(ABOVE)
Rocky mountain goat.

(RIGHT)
*Athabasca Falls,
Jasper National Park.*

their numbers are not high. Black bears are much
more common, and are often found scavenging by
roadsides or in campsites. Occasional reports are
made of attacks on humans, but this is far from a
common occurence. The parks protect at least two
endangered species, the bighorn sheep and the
grey wolf, and other mammals include moose,
wapiti, mule deer and mountain goat. Over 280
species of birds have been identified within the
parks, although most visit only during the summer
months. Two of the birds of prey that find
protection here are the golden eagle and the bald
eagle, which have seriously declined in numbers
across the continent.

This is one of the most heavily visited
protected areas in the world, and there are
numerous problems confronting the parks'
management. Several major highways and the
Trans-Canada railway transect much of the area.
Problems associated with the proximity of such
major arteries include road (and rail) kills, littering,
noise pollution, exhaust emissions, the spread of
weeds, and, of course, high levels of human
visitation with all of its implications.

Grizzly bear -
Ursus arctos horribilis.

DINOSAUR
PROVINCIAL PARK

Canada's Dinosaur Provincial Park is famous above all for the range and quality of dinosaur fossils which have been found there and which give the park its name. The remains of sixty-odd species from seven dinosaur families, including every known species from the Cretaceous Period (Coluridae, Hadrasauridae, Ornithomimidae, Tyrannosauridae, Nodosauridae, Ceratopsidae and Pachycephalosauridae) have so far been recovered in the park, as well as fossilized remains of other ancient animals including fish, reptiles, amphibians, and marsupials, which today are found chiefly in Australia. These invaluable fossils were unearthed from geological formations created around seventy-five million years ago, at the end of the Mesozoic Era. During this time, the park's slowly undulating rivers ran into the Bearpan Sea, where fluvial deposits settled in the shallow waters, merging into the clay shale and sandstone geological strata which forms the site of the park.

The park is also famous for its 'badlands', an austere yet beautiful sequence of buttes, mesas, natural tunnels, and 'hoodoos', or rock columns sculpted by erosion, which are reminiscent of the 'Fairy Chimneys' of Cappadocia, Turkey. The effect of this starkly-defined, atmospheric landscape is arresting, its bleak allure accentuated by moaning winds, cool air and wide skies.

The 'badlands' shelter plants which have adapted to its erosion-contoured, wind-swept terrain such as Sagebrush. On the larger sections of hillside are open stretches of grasslands. The Red Deer and Judith Rivers cut their way through the buttes and hills, forming river terraces that shelter stands of willow and cottonwood, whilst pockets of wetlands abut the rivers themselves.

Due to its grasslands, and winters which are usually less than harsh, Dinosaur Provincial Park is able to sustain large herds of white-tailed and mule deer as well as pronghorn, or American antelope, which is capable of attaining speeds of up to 47 miles per hour (75 kilometers per hour), in spite of being related to the sheep. The pronghorn is also unusual in that it sheds the outer shell of its antelope-like horns every year. Although it once roamed much of North America in enormous numbers, this tan and white animal was decimated by hunting and is now rarely sighted outside parks and reserves.

The park's bird life includes many birds of prey such as the golden eagle; the prairie falcon; the ferruginous hawk; the merlin; and the masked loggerhead shrike.

Aside from its famous fossil remains, fossil fuels have also been discovered in Dinosaur Provincial Park. In addition to three existing gas wells, there has also been a major gas development proposal made concerning a part of the park outside the 'Badlands' region. Any decision to go ahead with gas exploration and exploitation would not only have to meet stringent controls set by the national park, but might also have to deal with claims to the region by indigenous groups. Archeological finds proving prior inhabitation by native 'Plains Indian' cultures include a sequence of tepee rings, stone effigies and the location of a Vision Quest site. Regardless of whether or not natural gas exploitation goes ahead, the controlled grazing, which until now has occurred to the north of the Red Deer River, is to be abandoned.

- There are many predatory bird species including the golden eagle; the prairie falcon; the ferruginous hawk; the merlin; and the loggerhead shrike.

FACILITIES

Tourist facilities include a campsite, restaurant and picnic areas. The nearby town of Brooks also has many facilities. Tours to some of the fossil sites can be made, and there are many hiking trails, as well as a visitor education center inside the park.

(ABOVE) Dinosaur's famous badlands.

(LEFT) Golden eagle.

(FAR LEFT) Merlin.

GROS MORNE
NATIONAL PARK

Gros Morne is one of Canada's most magnificent national parks. Lying along the north eastern extremity of the Appalachian Mountains, within the provinces of Newfoundland and Labrador, its awe-inspiring scenery embraces the dramatic transition from the sea through to the vertical walls of land-locked fiords. It is the unique geological features of the park that ensure it a valued place among the natural treasures of our planet.

The field of earth science has made enormous advances in the past twenty years, with various dynamic theories restructuring our knowledge of the earth's geological history. One theory, that of plate tectonics, contends that the earth's crust consists of large plates which continually move and reform. While modern ocean crust is less than 200 million years old, the Appalachian Mountains contain evidence of plate tectonics that took place 600 - 400 million years ago. During that period rocks were transported hundreds of miles westward and assembled on the eastern edge of North America, and these stacked thrust slices are exposed in near-pristine condition in Gros Morne National Park.

The park's rock formations preserve many unusual geographic features. For example, the cliffs of Western Brook Pond display large vertical cracks which were caused by the separation of Europe and North America, together with their solidified contents of basaltic magma which are 600 million years old. There are also sedimentary strata that contain examples of evolution from mid-Cambrian through to mid-Ordovician times; an excellent exposure of the ancient contact between pre-Cambrian granites and gnosses; and Cambrian sea floor sedimentary rocks. Around the Green Gardens area of the park the pillow lavas and ash layers of a 'hot spot volcano' remain. The Tablelands area is comprised of blocks of ancient ocean crust and mantle (known as ophiolites) and has been called the 'Eighth Wonder of the World'. Gros Morne National Park also contains an inter-

nationally significant occurrence of xonotlite, a rare metamorphic mineral.

Other important geological features of the park can be found in the Cow Head Group, a display of well preserved easily accessible conglomerates of exceptional coarseness. More recently there have been forces such as glacial activity during the Pleistocene epoch. It was during this time that the park's magnificent fiords were created, the most spectacular being Western Brook Pond.

Although this park is primarily significant for its geological marvels, it also contains an interesting variety of flora and fauna. Scientists have noted 36 different vegetation types within the park, ranging from stunted coastal forest, peat

• The park contains a high proportion of rare or unique species in communities, for example the plant communities which grow on the soils of the tablelands area.
• There is also yellow birch, black ash, eastern white pine and red maple around Bonne Bay, while the alpine bearberry grows in the Long Range Mountains.

FAUNA

• Native fauna inhabiting the park include the little brown bat, arctic hare, beaver, muskrat, meadow vole, red fox, black bear, ermine, river otter, lynx and caribou, while others have been introduced including moose, American mink, snowshoe hare, red squirrel and masked shrew.
• There are over 230 species of birdlife associated with the park, and it is an important haven for migratory shore birds. Harlequin ducks, blackpoll warbler and arctic and common terns all have breeding sites within the park's grounds.

FACILITIES

In addition to 80mi (120km) of paved roads a system of hiking trails allows access to more remote areas. A number of campsites, with a total of 240 site emplacements, are located in the park, and hotels and other services are available in the adjacent communities. Information is available at a number

lands, sand dunes, salt marshes, sea cliffs, tundra, boreal forest and aquatic communities. Within these groups, there are 750 vascular species of flora, and 321 species of mosses and liverworts, representing over 60% of the known flora of Newfoundland. The park contains a high proportion of rare or unique species in communities, for example the plant communities which grow on the soils of the tablelands area. There is also yellow birch, black ash, eastern white pine and red maple around Bonne Bay, while the alpine bearberry grows in the Long Range Mountains.

Native fauna inhabiting the park include the little brown bat, arctic hare, beaver, muskrat, meadow vole, red fox, black bear, ermine, river otter, lynx and caribou, while others have been introduced including moose, American mink, snowshoe hare, red squirrel and masked shrew. A number of exotic species have been introduced, to the detriment of the indigenous fauna, nevertheless, protection since 1973 has seen populations increase, with the exception of American marten, which has disappeared from the park.

In the Atlantic Ocean adjoining the park one can view an incomparable assortment of marine life including pilot, minke and finback whales, and harbor seals. The icy waters of the park contain Atlantic salmon and arctic char with certain lakes containing highly unusual varieties of these fishes. There are over 230 species of birdlife associated with the park, and it is an important haven for migratory shore birds. Harlequin ducks, blackpoll warbler and arctic and common terns all have breeding sites within the park's grounds.

of sites, including the administrative and visitor reception center in Rocky Harbor. Facilities are also available for outdoor activities. One concession-run boat tour operates.

(ABOVE) Harbour seals.

(RIGHT) A pair of caribou bulls sparring.

(FAR RIGHT) Lynx.

1,000 species of flora have been recorded in Nahanni National Park.

The park is home to many animals associated with the 'Frozen North', that kind of wild, Jack London-like landscape which Nahanni, with its dramatic mixture of freezing winters, isolated territory and rough terrain, so powerfully evokes, including the grey wolf, the grizzly bear, and the black bear. Few animals have produced as many legends, and been so feared, as the wolf. For centuries dreaded by travellers and prospectors, hunters and trappers, isolated farmers and herdsmen, the wolf has suffered a savage decline in numbers, partly due to a campaign of deliberate extermination and partly due to loss of habitat caused by clearing, cultivation and the establishing of settlements. Nahanni's grey wolf population travels mainly in packs at night, and feeds on the park's substantial herds of moose, woodland caribou and white-tailed deer. The park is one of its last refuges in North America.

The grizzly bear is another animal which suffered great population loss, in its case hunted almost to extinction because it was so greatly valued as 'a trophy', being considered by presidents and common folk alike as the most impressive of all of North America's 'big game'. The grizzly can often be sighted close to one of Nahanni's many streams, fishing for Dolly Varden Trout. Also along the park's brooks can be found Canada's national animal, the beaver. In the high country are mountain goat; peregrine falcon; golden eagle; and bald eagle. Some 170 species of birds from 29 families have been recorded, including the elegant trumpeter swan.

Although hunting has been banned, this does not apply to the region's indigenous native people, who carry on their traditional hunting and fishing. A harmonious balance for the moment seems to have been struck between these people, the landscape they have inhabited for generations, and park and government authorities. However, mining of the mineral-rich lands just outside the national park could eventually result in heavy-metal run-offs into park waters, affecting their fabled purity and disturbing this hard-won equilibrium.

- Dense stands of spruce, poplar, black spruce and larch occur in valley bottoms and on northern slopes, while the highest ground possesses grass, lichens, sedges, and shrubs.
- There is an abundance of many beautiful wildflowers including golden rod, yellow monkey-flower and aster.

FAUNA

- Grey wolf and grizzly bear have both sought refuge here.
- There are substantial herds of moose, woodland caribou and white tailed deer.
- Along the many streams and rivers can be found the beaver as well as many salmonid fish, including Dolly Varden trout.
- Amongst the 170 species of bird recorded are the peregrine falcon, the golden and bald eagles, and the trumpeter swan.

FACILITIES

The administration office for the park is located in Fort Simpson, NWT. The park is visited mainly by experienced trekkers and campers. Its relative proximity to the Arctic Circle means that campers ought to be cautious about weather conditions, even in summer. Entry into the region is easiest by plane.

EL VIZCAINO

LOCATION

Central Baja California, between the Gulf of California and the Pacific Ocean, N 25° 22' to 28° 00', W 112° 14' to 115° 16'.

AREA

1,332,000ac (554,898ha).

FEATURES

- Every winter large numbers of blue whale, grey whale, harbor seal, northern elephant seal, and Californian sea lion come to these warm sheltered coastal lagoons for refuge and to breed.

FLORA

The vegetation is representative of arid environments with 'sarcocaul' shrubland, characterized by trees and shrubs of large trunk dimensions, 'crasicaul' shrubland, characterized by a predominance of cacti, and 'sarcocrasicaul' shrubland, with a mixture of both of the above with a predominance of candelabra forms.

FAUNA

- The fauna is relatively rich, with 299 species of terrestrial vertebrates having been recorded, including four amphibian species, 43 reptiles, 182 birds and 35 mammals.
- Notable mammals include a relict population of pronghorn antelope, mule deer, desert bighorn, kit fox, Baja Californian rock squirrel and deer mouse.

Every winter this reserve plays host to one of nature's most spectacular events. Large numbers of grey whale, harbor seal, northern elephant seal, and Californian sea lion come to these warm sheltered coastal lagoons for refuge and to breed. It is here that some of the most exciting opportunities exists to view these graceful giants of the sea at close quarters.

Located in the central part of the Baja California peninsula, this site comprises three separate areas; San Ignacio Lagoon, Ojo de Liebre Lagoon and Sierra de San Francisco. The eastern topography is dominated by the main mountain range of Baja California with heights ranging up to 6,600ft (2,000m), while the Pacific coast has three isolated ranges (Sierra Vizcaino) extending along it, with heights up to 6,000ft (1,840m). There is a series of shallow sandy bays, inlets and lagoons in the extreme northwest and to the south. The entire area is very arid, with less than 4in (100mm) of rain falling each year. Summers are very hot, with temperatures reaching 113°F (45°C).

The vegetation is representative of arid environments with 'sarcocaul' shrubland, characterized by trees and shrubs of large trunk dimensions, 'crasicaul' shrubland, with a predominance of cacti, and 'sarcocrasicaul' shrubland, characterized by a mixture of both of the above with a predomi-

nance of candelabra forms. Other vegetation includes perennial herbs growing on sandbanks, areas dominated by salt tolerant species and shrublands with non-spiny deciduous leaved plants. There are also communities of Yucca, mangroves and a small area of conifer forest which harbors numerous endemics.

The fauna is relatively rich, with 299 species of terrestrial vertebrates having been recorded, including four amphibian species, 43 reptiles, 182 birds and 35 mammals. Notable mammals include a relict population of pronghorn antelope, mule deer, desert bighorn, kit fox, Baja Californian rock squirrel and deer mouse. There are numerous species of marine mammals known to frequent the waters, including the increasingly rare blue whale, as well as grey whales, harbor seals, Californian sea lions and northern elephant seals. Four species of marine turtle are threatened - leatherback, green turtle, hawksbill and Olive Ridley.

The lagoons are an important refuge for wintering wildfowl - 10% of the wildfowl wintering on the west coast of Mexico winter in the reserve, including over 70,000 Brent geese, which is 63% of Mexico's winter population. Notable birds endemic to the peninsula include yellowthroat and black-fronted hummingbird, whilst threatened species include American white pelican, sandhill crane, bald eagle, golden eagle, osprey, peregrine falcon, common caracara and burrowing owl.

There are a number of important prehistoric sites on the peninsula, as well as petroglyphs, wall paintings and ancient ruins. There is also much early evidence of European colonization, including Puerto Santa Cruz (now La Paz) which was established in 1533 at the extreme south of the peninsula.

There are some serious management problems evident in the reserve, including commercial salt extraction, large scale mining, oil drilling, unsustainable turtle and fishery exploitation, and hunting.

(LEFT) Kit fox.

- There are 26 marine mammal species, including grey whales, harbor seals, Californian sea lions and northern elephant seals. Four species of marine turtle are threatened - leatherback, green turtle, hawksbill and Olive Ridley.
- The lagoons are an important refuge for wintering wildfowl - 10% of the wildfowl wintering on the west coast of Mexico winter in the reserve.
- Notable birds endemic to the peninsula include yellowthroat and black-fronted hummingbird, whilst threatened species include American white pelican, sandhill crane, bald eagle, golden eagle, osprey, peregrine falcon, common caracara and burrowing owl.

FACILITIES

La Paz and Tijuana are both accessible by air, and there are road links from these centers to the reserve. Facilities are available in the towns of Guerrero Negro and Santa Rosalia. There is organized whale watching at Ojo de Liebre Lagoon. Tourism is being strictly controlled with visitor numbers being gradually decreased. There are two wardens permanently employed in the reserve.

(ABOVE) Two male elephant seals battling in the surf.

(LEFT) A female Ridley's turtle preparing her nest.

SIAN KA'AN

This Caribbean coastal reserve of 1,267,200ac (528,000ha) lies in the south-east of Mexico, along the eastern part of the Yucatan Peninsula, in the state of Quintana Roo. Sian Ka'an includes a marine reserve bounded by a magnificent barrier reef, which is part of the second longest coral reef system in the world. The reef considerably diminishes the destructiveness of the waves during the violent storms often experienced in this part of the Caribbean.

The terrestrial part of the reserve sits on a recently-emerged limestone plain. Here there are sand dunes, freshwater and saltwater marshes, and mangrove swamps, as well as closed canopy flood forest and semi-evergreen forests. Although there is a rarity of surface running water, Sian Ka'an is notable for the presence of sink holes, or 'cenotes', shallow karst wells, often between 165 to 330ft (50 to 100m) in diameter, that give access to subterranean channels of water which, because of its hardness, is remarkably clear. As the water table is always close to the surface, Sian Ka'an is often subjected to flooding, especially during the wet season, when more than 70% of the land is underwater.

The wet season is from May to October, when the easterly winds prevail. Cyclones occur during this period, as do 'mangueras'- marine tornados -which can cause brief but violent havoc. The wet season corresponds with summer, when temperatures have been known to reach in excess of 112°F (40°C), and the flood waters simmer under overcast skies. During the dry season, when northerly winds sometimes reach gale force, the ground quickly dries, aided by the high salinity of the soil. Then 'Petenes', raised wooded islands often with palms up to 50ft (15m) high, seem to eerily emerge from the flood waters. The semi-evergreen forests, occupying the highest ground, occur in the non-flood areas of the reserve and encompass about 30% of the total land area.

In such variant conditions, a fascinating range of wildlife occurs. Five different types of wild cat can be found in Sian Ka'an: the jaguar; the puma, and three smaller cats. The first of these, the ocelot, is also known as both the leopard cat and the tiger cat because the brown markings on its yellowish hide are neither spots nor stripes, but something in between. It's only 28in (70cm) long, and hunts birds, reptiles and small mammals. The second of these smaller wild cats is the margay, or tigrillo, a nocturnal hunter. The last one is the jaguarundi, a long-bodied, short-legged cat, with a coat that varies from red-brown to dark grey.

Although there has never been an accurate inventory taken, it is believed that the reserve is frequented by over 350 species of bird, with about two thirds of them using Sian Ka'an as a breeding ground, particularly wading and marine birds. Among the more common species are flamingo; spoonbill; cormorants; and frigate birds. Reptiles include the crocodile and four species of turtle: green; loggerhead; leatherback; and hawksbill. The marine reserve contains over fifty recorded species of fish, as well as sharks, and decapods such as lobsters.

There is a coastal belt nearly 44mi (70km) long where limited agricultural exploitation is permitted, carried out by local people of Mayan decent operating out of twenty five small 'ranchos' or holdings. Here, copra is harvested, and subsistence hunting and the gathering of some species of plant life is allowed. The indiscriminate logging of red and white cedar and mahogany has been stopped but not before nearly completely eradicating those species from the reserve.

A concern to the reserve's management is the growth of tourism on the coast immediately north of Sian Ka'an. The first influx of tourists arrived over twenty years ago, attracted to the Tulum beaches, and today the area is one of the most frequented tourist areas in Mexico, and there are plans to greatly increase tourist traffic in the Cancun/Tulum area. As the numbers of both tourists and new arrivals attracted to working in service industries grew in the eighties, facilities could not keep up. The most serious environmental problem so far encountered has been damage

(ABOVE) Tayra.

(LEFT) Geoffroy's spider monkey.

(FAR LEFT) Ocelot.

caused by untreated sewage polluting the reserve's waters, and the slow but steady infiltration of tourists into the reserve itself. Because of the fragility of the reserve's unique ecosystem, any large scale increase in tourism so close to its waters would have a detrimental impact.

To Save our Heritage is to Save the Earth

We live with the land, the sea, and the sky. This home, our Earth, is the repository of our heritage we are now called upon to save.

Humankind's exploitation of the Earth's resources has yielded a burden of damage fast tampering with the planet's life-sustaining gifts.

In a wisp of time, the great herds of roaming beasts and the exotic creatures of nature's awesome genius, have been corralled into preserves, or placed on exhibition.

We have witnessed a rainfall of burning water, a shower of acid, corroding green to brown and converting lakes into dead pools. Entire landscapes of ancient forests, wetlands and tall grass prairies have disappeared. Deserts encroach on land stripped of vegetation. A spasm of species extinction is occurring within a blink of biological time as swathes of tropical rainforests vanish. Ultraviolet radiation streaming through a breach in the ozone shield may already be diminishing the phyto-plankton base of the marine food chain. Coral reefs around the world are inexplicably dying. Evidence is mounting that global warming is already under way. The air in our cities is polluted. Hardly any of us live in a place clean of toxins contaminating some part of the land or water. Each year 100 million more of us lay claim to the resources being so treated.

We are altering the Earth's biological integrity. And we are doing so at an ever increasing rate of frenzy.

The admonition to care for the land is a common theme of our ethical inheritance. The American Indian and oriental wisdom express the idea as living as one, in harmony with the land. Our Judeo Christian heritage speaks of stewardship, a holding in trust for those who are to follow.

Early in this century these concepts took political shape in the formation of the conservation movement. The impetus then was to preserve nature's most wondrous creations, to set aside from humankind's changing hand what was beautiful and wild.

Later as awareness grew of the scope of our collective effect upon the resources that maintain life, an evolution took place into the movement we now know as environmentalism.

The evolution has most recently gone beyond grasping the breadth of the challenges, to realizing their urgency. Incremental steps to redress accretions of degradation are no longer sufficient. At issue is the immediate health of the planet and those who occupy it. In a few short decades the quest to preserve pieces at the margin has escalated into the imperative to forestall collapse.

Environmentalism may no longer be defined as an endeavor to protect aspects for the future. Today's environmentalism has become the necessity to preserve health, our own and the planet's, for survival in the present.

Environmentalism draws its inspiration from the ethical impulse to care for the land, to act with prudence in our use of the Earth's bounty. The indispensable corollary to this belief is that environmentalism begins with the individual. The life of environmentalism is wholly dependent on the choices individuals make, the actions they pursue to give meaning to their beliefs. The conviction that each one of us can make a difference is at the root of the environmental movement. Environmentalism is fundamentally a personal responsibility.

At the exact moment the individual might feel most daunted in face of enormous challenges, a tremendous opportunity presents itself to reorganize the vitality of our collective energies toward healing the damage to our planet.

This effort will require us to look past the old alliances based on fear and conflict toward the realization of our interdependent common interests. Just as no one is truly safe as long as another is allowed to suffer injustice, so too, no part of our environment is truly healthy so long as we allow despoliation to occur elsewhere. Individuals must magnify their concern for the environment in new alliances that unite, rather than divide, the North and South, the East and West, the industrialized and the developing world. The engines of economic competitiveness must be retuned so that they generate sustainable growth and development instead of devouring our patrimony to the impoverishment of our children.

The task is huge. These are the aspirations of environmentalism: to educate and empower the individual, to reshape our understanding of global security and to forge the alliances that will create a sustainable future on an Earth at peace with itself.

This, environmentalists believe, is not just a vision, but a necessary choice for survival. On the success of our efforts rests whether environmental destruction will continue with unforeseen and possible tragic results, or if we will in fact preserve our heritage and save the Earth.

Dr. JAY D HAIR
President IUCN - The World Conservation Union and
The National Wildlife Federation, Washington, D.C.

The Grand Canyon.

EVERGLADES
NATIONAL PARK

Everglades lies on the southern tip of the Florida peninsula, which, although geologically young, is one of the more stable portions of the continent. Temperate and sub-tropical America meet here; land, sea and sky come together to form a complex biological system which links urban life with pristine wilderness and makes the park one of the greatest natural history and environmental centers on the planet. The fauna, and particularly the flora of south Florida have fascinated scientists and naturalists since colonization, and are the primary reason for the establishment of the park.

The park is actually a shallow basin, averaging only 4ft (1m) in depth, and never exceeding 10ft (3m). It is underlain by massive deposits of Pleistocene limestone - the waters of the bay being one of the most productive natural limestone 'factories' in the United States.

Located at a meeting point of several climatic zones, the park supports an enormously wide variety of flora and fauna. Naturally occurring fires, high rainfall, inland penetration by sea water and hurricanes all help determine the vegetation of the park. There is a superb array of bromeliads and orchids, over 1,000 kinds of seed bearing plants, and nearly 120 species of trees. These range from tropical species such as palms, mangroves, gumbo limbo, through to temperate species such as ash, mulberry and oaks, with even cactus and yucca thriving in certain areas. The preponderance of West Indian species is a particularly interesting feature.

Within the park's boundaries are five separate vegetative types. These are: hammocks, which are tree islands generally comprising mixed hardwoods; bayheads, or tree islands consisting of

isolated stands of specific species; pinelands, comprised predominantly of southern Florida slash pine; coastal mangrove; and sawgrass, a sedge covering lowland prairies to the north and eastwards. In addition, at least four different aquatic community types thrive in the park - the inland freshwater areas; the brackish water or estuarine areas where salt water merges with fresh; shallow shoreline and offshore bays; and the deeper gulf coastal waters. In addition, there is the area of transition from glade to mangrove. This is a rich and productive zone where pink shrimp, stone crab and spiny lobster flourish.

The landscape of Everglades abounds with a kaleidoscopic display of birdlife, with over 300 species recorded, many of which are rare or endangered. In fact, concern over the disappearance of nesting grounds for ibis, herons and other wading birds was one of the reasons behind the establishment of the park, and now these birds are gradually increasing in number. Other endangered birds finding protection in Everglades include peregrine falcon, Florida Everglade kite, southern

bald eagle, red-cockaded woodpecker and Cape Sable seaside sparrow.

Everglades is also a sanctuary for many mammals, such as the manatee, which is endemic to the park and depends upon it for its survival. Other threatened species include the Florida panther, the American alligator (now increasing after reaching the brink of extinction), the American crocodile, the Atlantic green turtle, the mangrove fox squirrel, the Miami black-headed snake, the Florida black bear and the Everglades mink.

The creation of Everglades was the culmination of many years of hard work. This began in the early part of the century when measures were taken to protect plume-bird rookeries. (Harvesting feathers was a lucrative trade, and in 1905 one of the warders was murdered at his post). Luckily, lack of funding did not deter concerned conservationists. They were becoming alarmed by the environmental destruction caused through drainage and canal building which had been undertaken to create more 'useable' land. Hurricanes, flooding, fires and salinization of water supplies resulted from the canal construction and drainage, and finally the public realized the vital need to maintain the delicate ecology of the region, and Everglades National Park was established.

Of course, protecting an area through legislation, although vital, is never enough on its own, and unfortunately Everglades today stands as a symbol of the destructive effects of human neglect. The threats to the integrity of this park are so grave that it was placed on the List of World Heritage in Danger by the World Heritage Committee in December 1993. Perhaps the most serious of these threats is posed by the rapid colonization of exotic plant species. There are at least 221 species of introduced plants occuring in the park, including the particularly notorious Australian tree known as paperbark which is clogging up the waterways at a brisk rate. Water management is another major environmental threat to the ecosystem. Water quality, timing of canal releases, amounts, and divergences affect the natural system that, in turn, controls wildlife and vegetation populations. Research is being undertaken to understand the flow of water and its effects on wild plants and animals in order to revise the hydrological management of the park.

(ABOVE) American
alligator.

(RIGHT) Osprey.

REDWOOD
NATIONAL PARK

REDWOOD NATIONAL PARK

LOCATION:

Pacific coast, northern California.
N 47° 29' to 48° 11',
W 123° 07' to 124° 42'.

AREA

102,000ac (42,400ha).

FEATURES

The tallest (468ft - 112m), second and third tallest trees on earth are in this park.

FLORA

- The floor of the forests is littered with ferns and small shrubs and above them is a thick understorey of smaller trees.
- Moving west, the altitude increases, the soil becomes drier and the redwoods disappear to be replaced by smaller forests of Douglas fir, Sitka spruce, western hemlock, grand fir, big-leaf maple and other species.

FAUNA

- Numerous mammals are to be found within these forests, including the Roosevelt elk, Columbian black-tailed deer, black bear, coyote, fox, bob cat, mountain beaver, skunk and the occasional mountain lion.
- The bird life is interesting and varied, with several rare and endangered species, including the spotted owl, southern bald eagle, American peregrine falcon and American osprey.

(ABOVE) Puma cub.

This area's primary significance lies in the coastal redwood forest which give Redwood National Park its name. These trees are at their most magnificent in the massive stands found alongside some of the park's larger streams, in particular the Smith River and Redwood Creeks, where one of these stands hosts the tallest tree on earth (468ft - 112m). Surprisingly, it is not easily visible, as the girth and height of the surrounding trees are so great as to obscure its dominance. The second and third tallest trees on the planet are also to be found within this park.

These silent giants have stood tall and defiant for centuries, patiently bearing mute witness to the frantic human activity that has surrounded them. And how frantic that activity has been! Large tracts of ancient virgin forest have been wiped out simply to satisfy mankind's ephemeral needs. More than half of the park has been logged, as well as almost the entire watershed upstream from the park. All remnant old growth stands outside the park will be cut during the next decade, and second growth harvests have begun on lands outside the park. Regional logging has been carried out on some of the world's most erodable soils. The redwood forests of this park represent just under half of all remaining old growth redwood stands, a small fragment of once extensive cover. There are only 38,000ac (15,800ha) of old growth redwood remaining in the park; 50,000ac (20,800ha) having been logged. Is there a more scandalous and shameful story of human greed and shortsightedness, than the story that these few remaining giants have to tell?

The park management is doing a highly commendable job with what is left. A watershed rehabilitation programme has been implemented to return the downstream portion of Redwood Creek drainage basin within the park to a reasonable facsimile of its natural state. A land rehabilitation scheme has been set up to protect the tallest known trees in the world by restoring those areas devastated by clearfelling.

The topography of the park encompasses low coastal mountains, heavily dissected by numerous streams and rivers. The area can be roughly divided into three major ecosystems: a narrow strip of Redwood forests, a marine/shoreline environment,

FACILITIES

Nearly 700,000 people visit the park annually and enjoy campgrounds, nature, hiking, horseback and bicycle trails, picnic grounds, information centers and scenic drives. In addition to US nationals, Canadians account for 4-5% of visits and overseas visitors for 0.3-0.9%.

(FAR RIGHT) This giant sequoia is called 'Washington tree'.

Californian sea lion.

and an area of coastal scrubland to the north. The forests are to be found at lower altitudes nearer to the coast. The floor of these forests is littered with ferns and small shrubs and above them is a thick understorey of smaller trees. Moving west, the altitude increases and the soil becomes drier. Consequently the redwoods disappear to be replaced by smaller forests of Douglas fir, Sitka spruce, western hemlock, grand fir, big-leaf maple and other species.

Numerous mammals are to be found within these forests, including the Roosevelt elk, Columbian black-tailed deer, black bear, coyote, fox, bob cat, mountain beaver, skunk and the occasional mountain lion. The bird life is interesting and varied, with several rare and endangered species, including the spotted owl, southern bald eagle, American peregrine falcon and American osprey.

The coastal scrubland acts intermittently as an area of transition from the forests to the marine environment. It is dominated by low growing trees, woody shrubs and herbaceous plants. The coastal environs are diverse, encompassing 35mi (56km) of beaches, coastal prairies, rocky cliffs and brushland. Secluded coves, beaches and offshore rocks provide havens and important breeding sites for many sea birds as well as seals and sea lions. The coastal waters often play host to elephant seals and grey whales, both potentially threatened species.

The numerous creeks and rivers of the park abound in fish, particularly rainbow trout and steelhead salmon, which move seasonally in from sea and up the streams for spawning. Other species include lamprey, candlefish and two rare species of sturgeon. The numerous marshes and ponds provide ideal nesting and feeding sites for several species of migratory water fowl.

Several important archeological sites have been uncovered in the park, some dating as far back as 300BC. These include semi-subterranean plank houses, sweat houses, cemeteries, hearths and middens. These remains have yielded invaluable insights into the customs and rituals of these early riverine forest dwelling societies.

Unfortunately the awe inspiring redwood forests of this park are but a tiny remnant of what once stood along the west coast before the development of the timber extraction industry. Other proposed developments such as offshore oil and gas development, mining and subdivisions also pose serious threats to the park. It is against this sombre and tragic background that we view Redwood National Park as a symbol not just of the urgent need to preserve what we have left on this planet, but also of the dire consequences of thoughtless 'development'.

YELLOWSTONE
NATIONAL PARK

YELLOWSTONE
NATIONAL PARK.

LOCATION

NW corner of Wyoming
and adjacent areas of
Montana and Idaho,
N 44° 08' to 45° 07',
W 109° 10' to
111° 10'.

AREA

2,156,000ac
(898,349ha).

FEATURES

- In 1872 Yellowstone
  was declared the
  world's first national
  park.
- Yellowstone is most
  famous for its
  spectacular hot
  springs and geysers,
  the most famous of
  these being Old
  Faithful.
- About half of
  Yellowstone is
  covered by water.

FLORA

- The park is 80%
  forested, and 80% of
  that is dominated by
  lodgepole pine
- Great elevational
  differences produce a
  range of plant
  communities, from
  semi-arid steppe to
  alpine tundra.
- Seven species of
  coniferous trees and
  nearly 1,100 species
  of vascular plants
  grow in the park.

FAUNA

- Yellowstone park has
  the only continuously
  wild free-ranging
  bison in the U.S.
  whose numbers are
  naturally regulated.
- Other ungulates are
  elk, mule deer,
  moose, pronghorn,
  and bighorn sheep.

In 1872, United States Congress set aside nearly 2,160,000ac (900,000ha) of land as a 'public park and pleasure ground', with President Ulysses S. Grant signing the Yellowstone Act on March 1 of that year. That historic act made Yellowstone the world's first national park.

Yellowstone National Park borders three states; the north-west corner of Wyoming and adjacent areas in Montana and Idaho. Its unique beauty derives largely from early volcanic activity, and the oldest exposed rocks in Yellowstone date back 2.7 billion years. The world's largest volcanic crater (or caldera) was formed here approximately 600,000 years ago. At 1,200sqmi (3,110sqkm), this caldera is 100 times larger than that of Krakatoa and covers half the park. Within it lies a singular phenomenon- the petrified remains of 27 different forests, each successively buried by volcanic

eruptions which began 50 million years ago. These forests comprised sycamore, walnut, magnolia, chestnuts, oaks and redwoods, and the majority of the trees are still in their upright position.

Today, Yellowstone is forested largely by five species of conifers, the most prolific being lodgepole pine.

Yellowstone is most famous for its spectacular hot springs and geysers. Hot springs form when heat from the magma chamber inside the earth transmits into the surrounding rock, thus heating the ground water which then rises to the surface as hot springs. If access to the earth's surface is restricted however, the temperature and pressure increase and form geysers. There are at least 200 geysers within the park, with about 60 reaching ten feet (three meters) or more in height. The most famous of these is undoubtedly Old Faithful.

IGUAZU
AND
IGUAÇU
NATIONAL PARKS

LOCATION

ARGENTINA: Less than 3mi (5km) from the Paraguay border in Misiones Province, northern Argentina, the Iguazu River forms the northern boundary of both the reserve and park, and also the southern boundary of Iguaçu National Park in Brazil,
S 25° 32' to 25° 45',
W 54° 33' to 54° 10'.
BRAZIL: Parana State, lying along part of the Argentinian border, and close to that with Paraguay,
S 25° 00' to 25° 45',
W 53° 43' to 54° 30'.

AREA

ARGENTINA:
132,000ac (55,000ha).
BRAZIL: 408,000ac (170,000ha).

FEATURES

The falls, spanning the border between Brazil and Argentina, form a spectacular semicircular front of 9,000ft (2,700m). The average height of the falls is 240ft (72m), and the falls themselves are made up of well-over 150 subsidiary falls. At

These two national parks appear on the World Heritage List as separate listings, as nominated by their respective countries, but represent a contiguous whole. The area possesses a large expanse of dense rainforest and is famous for its spectacular, fan-shaped waterfalls. The Iguazu/Iguaçu river forms the boundary of both the national parks and their respective countries.

The falls are located where the Iguazu river tumbles down the edge of the Southern Brazilian Plateau, forming a vast, curving wall of water, nearly 2mi (3km) long, of which nearly a third lies within Brazil, the remainder in Argentina. The average height of the falls is 240ft (72m), and the falls themselves are made up of well over 150 subsidiary falls. At its height, the flow rate is an impressive 234,000 cubic feet per second (6,500 cubic meters per second), ensuring the roar from the falls is audible for many miles (kilometers). Just beyond the falls, the Iguazu/Iguaçu river turns through an abrupt canyon less than 330ft (100m) wide: a tectonic crack that has been enlarged over thousands of years by erosion. Studded throughout the falls are dozens of islands and islets, some no more than rocks. On many of these is found a unique species of flora which can only flourish in the atmosphere of constant vapor and spray which the falls provide.

The unique interdependency found in subtropical rainforest is particularly evident in these parks. The upper strata is formed by the giants, growing to heights of over 100ft (30m), their branches interlocking and forming the famous rainforest canopy. Up there in the sunlight is a world that has never been properly chartered, where strange animals which have adapted to the environment, such as tree frogs and gliding snakes, can be found. As every two days the world loses an area of forest around the size of these parks, it is

certain that thousands of species which have flourished for countless years in the rainforest canopies will be eradicated without ever having been recorded; extinct not only in fact but even in memory.

The giant trees, such as the palo rosa and the rabo, provide access to the sunlight for climbing plants, whilst below them is the next strata, the intermediate trees which require less sunlight than the giants. Below these are stands of bamboo, and then the high ferns and shrubs; while in the dank shade of the low ferns, amidst a world of damp,

decaying organic matter, grow fungi, mosses and algae: every species accepting its place within a different strata according to its needs, an ideal example of a multifarious, interdependent society.

The parks' most famous animal is the jaguar, a more powerful and less gainly wildcat than its cousin, the leopard, which is also found here. An excellent fisher and swimmer, and a superb climber, the jaguar is well-suited to the environment. Unhappily all its abilities have not been enough to save it from being hunted nearly to extinction. Once highly coveted by big game hunters who

greatly valued it as a 'trophy', its pelt, which is now banned in most countries, still fetches enormous prices. The jaguar's loud cry, made only at night when it penetrates the jungle, is both hair-raising and unforgettable, but sadly is nowadays rarely ever heard.

Apart from the jaguar and leopard, there are three smaller wildcats which roam the rainforests: the tiger-cat; the jaguarundi, which bears little resemblance to its namesake; and the ocelot. Other animals found include the giant anteater, and its tree-dwelling cousin, the tamandua; the tapir, a

its height, the flow rate is an impressive 234,000 cubic feet per second (6,500 cubic meters per second), ensuring the roar from the falls is audible for many miles.

- The unique interdependency found in subtropical rainforest is particularly evident in Iguazu. The upper strata is formed by the giants, growing to heights of over 100ft (30m), their branches interlocking and forming the famous rainforest canopy.

- The giant trees, such as the palo rosa and the rabo, provide access to the sunlight for climbing plants, whilst below them is the next strata, the intermediate trees, below these are stands of bamboo, and then the high ferns and shrubs; while in the dank shade of the low ferns, amidst a world of damp, decaying organic matter, grow fungi, mosses and algae.

FAUNA

- The park's most famous animal is the jaguar, a more powerful and less gainly wildcat than its cousin, the leopard, which is also found here.

- There are also three smaller wildcats which roam the rainforests: the tiger-cat; the jaguarundi and the ocelot.

- Other animals found in Iguazu include the giant anteater, and its tree-dwelling cousin, the tamandua; the tapir, margay, brocket deer, American tapir, bush dog, capybara and usutu viper, the crab-eating raccoon, and its cousin, the coati; and La Plata otter.

An iguana is this ocelot's prey.

long-snouted distant relative of the horse which is believed to be one of the oldest of all mammal species; the crab-eating raccoon, and its cousin, the coati; and La Plata otter. Of the nearly 300 bird species catalogued here, more than half are residents including the toco toucan; the pygmy owl and the ringed kingfisher. The many monkeys present in the forests include capuchin and black howler.

The most immediate threat to Iguazu comes from poachers, who take advantage of the relatively easy access which national highways, that pass through both the national park proper and the adjacent reserve, afford. This, together with satellite-linked telephones, means that poachers can be dropped off at one point and

picked up several days later in an entirely different location, thus more easily avoiding capture. The falls themselves are currently menaced by Brazilian plans for extensive up-river damming, the effects of which would be wide-ranging and almost certainly adverse.

- Of the nearly 300 bird species catalogued at Iguazu, more than half are residents including the toco toucan; the pygmy owl and the ringed kingfisher.
- The many monkeys present in the forests include capuchin and black howler.

FACILITIES

Iguazu, like its northern neighbor is heavily visited, with over a third of a million visitors a year. There is a wide range of facilities in the town of Puerto Iguazu, including an international airport, hotels, restaurants and camping grounds; while there are hotels, restaurants and picnic areas at the falls themselves. Helicopters can be chartered to fly over the falls from the Brazilian side, affording an unforgettable sight but also creating such a racket, they can even be heard over the roar of the falls themselves. Boat trips and a few nature trails are also available. In Brazil,the park receives over one million visitors each year, and the load is spread quite evenly throughout the year. It is well served by roads, and is close to an airport. There is a large hotel within the park, a heliport, a museum, access roads, trails, and sightseeing spots. Interpretive trails and a visitor center are under development.

(LEFT) Toucan.

LOS GLACIARES
NATIONAL PARK

Los Glaciares is one of the most dazzling, and unusual, of all the world's natural sites. The heart of this 1,070,000ac (445,900ha) national park, created back in 1937, is a stretch of glaciers 220mi (350km) long, with a width that varies from 25 to 45mi (40 to 70km). Known as the 'Campo de Hielo Patagonico' or Patagonian Ice Field, this glacier sequence of over 15,000sqmi (14,000sqkm) is the largest ice mantle in the world outside of Antarctica; its attraction for visitors being, of course, that it is immensely more accessible. Highlighted by the distant peaks of the Andean Cordillera, the ice fields in summer ripple with the glitter of sunlight, a luminous world hued with blue reflected from the sky and the region's lakes and waterways. The air, dense with cold and hazed with the shimmer of ice particles whenever the wind lifts, often resounds with the boom of icebergs splitting from ice shelves, a terrifying yet exhilarating sound which echoes across the water.

This glacier activity is concentrated around two main bodies of water: Lago Argentino, with a system of finger lakes to its west, and its northern neighbor, Lago Viedma. Both lakes, formed from ancient glacial origin, flow into the Atlantic Ocean via the Santa Cruz River. To the west of the lakes rises the Andean Cordillera, shadowing the border with Chile. Its highest point is Mount Fitzroy, at just under 11,500ft (3,500m), which also represents the northernmost reach of the park.

The most fascinating of the park's 47 glaciers is Moreno, one of the few glaciers left in the world not in retreat. Creeping slowly forward, it periodically blocks the waterway known as the 'Canal de los Tempanos' (canal of icebergs), until the water held back by the ice exerts such enormous pressure that this naturally-formed dam explodes, showering the surrounding area with particles of ice. The Canal de los Tempanos connects Lago Argentino with one of its most southern finger lakes, Brazo Rico. The Magallanes Peninsula, a coin-shaped piece of land about 13mi (20km) across, is a perfect spot for watching iceberg and glacier activity, surrounded as it is on three sides by Brazo Rico, the

Canal de los Tempanos, and Lago Argentino itself.

The park has two distinct types of vegetation, Patagonian steppe and subantarctic Patagonian forest which includes large stands of beech. Guaytecas Islands cypress, which was once threatened with extinction, has been successfully reintroduced. Up until recently, the park was suffering serious damage to its steppe lands, due to overgrazing of livestock, particularly by sheep. Mount Fitzroy in particular has suffered in the past. In an effort to control both sheep and cattle grazing in the national park, a reserve of 370,000ac (154,100ha), which acts as a buffer zone, was created. Although the park itself is uninhabited,

threats have receded with the development of park management plans, but serious problems remain. Recent highways have opened the area to settlement and land clearing. The completion of the Chiriqui-Bocas del Toro oil pipeline in 1988 involved construction of an adjacent highway, which opened the forests of Bocos del Toro province for the first time to settlement, logging and cattle grazing. Since 1981 there has been continual encroachment, including a new road to a communication facility built on the summit and a proposal for a new road across the park to connect the towns of Cerro Punta and Boquete. Clearing of land and fires remain a serious and increasing problem and have caused severe erosion particularly on the southern and eastern slopes.

A young jaguar.

Biodiversity
- the Wealth of Our World

THE PLANET Earth is blessed with a great diversity of genes, species, habitats, cultures, and ecosystems. This biodiversity is the result of hundreds of millions of years of history, including drifting continents, changes in sea level, ice ages, volcanoes, and evolution.

More recent times have seen our species emerge as a dominant force in ecosystems throughout the world, with numerous local cultures earning a living from locally available resources. People have domesticated plants and animals, and are exerting increasing control over the landscape. The spread of major crops has changed the face of the Earth. Wheat from the Middle East, maize and potatoes from the Americas, rubber from Brazil, rice from tropical Asia, palm oil from Africa, and a small handful of others have replaced far more diverse systems, and have produced more for people. Combined with improved medical care, improved communications, fossil fuel energy, and greatly expanded industrial production, the growth in agricultural productivity has enabled the human population to increase to well over five billion. Our share of the planet's natural wealth has therefore expanded considerably. According to one estimate, almost 40 per cent of our planet's net primary terrestrial photosynthetic productivity is now directly consumed, diverted, or wasted as a result of human activities, a startling indication of how powerful our ecological influence has been.

Many people would say that major habitat changes and losses of biodiversity are the inevitable price we must pay for progress, as humans become an ever more dominant species on Earth. But in the late 20th century, many people are beginning to worry that we may be squandering the natural wealth which supports our way of life, and that resources which once were renewable are now being exhausted. Some scientists predict that, if present trends continue, up to 25 percent of the world's species will be lost in the next several decades, accompanied by an equally alarming degradation of habitats and ecosystems. Even worse, indications are that present trends in the loss of species and habitats are in fact accelerating. If projections on the growth of human populations and economic activities prove to be accurate, the loss of diversity could be so great as to undermine prospects for even the sustainable use of natural systems at present levels of production. What can be done to stem the loss?

The World Heritage Convention provides one of the most effective bastions against the onslaughts of human greed. It protects areas like Manu National Park in Peru, which by itself contains more species of plants and birds than all of North America; Serengeti National Park in Tanzania, the last place in the tropics where huge migrations of wildebeests and zebras can still be seen; Salonga National Park in Zaïre, with its vast expanses of tropical forests; and the Great Barrier Reef in Australia, where marine ecosystems in all their diversity continue to evolve.

World Heritage sites are also a symbolic expression of the way things ought to be: where governments make a statement about their commitment to conserve places with outstanding biodiversity. When the government of Cameroon adds a diverse tropical forest like Dja to the World Heritage List, it is making a political statement: its contribution to the world is biodiversity, not just logs to be shipped to market. Such statements are increasingly important in a time when most habitats are being over-exploited. World Heritage helps governments demonstrate that maintaining the productivity of natural ecosystems is one of their highest priorities, along with national defence, health, and education.

But there is no room for complacency. The World Heritage network still has large gaps, leaving much of the world's biodiversity still unprotected. The Amazon, Mexico, southern Africa, Indochina, and many marine habitats are still poorly represented. Even so, World Heritage provides one of the best available mechanisms to mobilize greater support for conserving areas containing outstanding examples of our planet's biological wealth.

JEFFREY A MCNEELY
Chief Conservation Officer, IUCN

FACILITIES

Most tourists who visit the Galapagos arrive aboard cruise ships, or on smaller, group-chartered boats. There are also flights from Quito which land on the island of San Cristobal. Boats can be hired on site. Within the archipelago, there are 27 areas designated as 'Intensive Visitor Zones', where a maximum of 90 people are allowed together at any one time. An additional 15 'Extensive Visitor Zones' are open to groups of less than 12. All visitors must follow specified trails when on land, and use guides within the visitor zones. The settlement of Puerto Ayora, on Santa Cruz, is perhaps the best land base, with hotels, shops and restaurants. From there one can take the famous walk to Tortuga Bay, visit sink holes and long lava tubes, and see giant Galapagos tortoises at the Charles Darwin Research Station.

(FAR LEFT ABOVE)
Land iguana.

(FAR LEFT BELOW)
Galapagos tortoise.

(LEFT) Prickly pear.

SANGAY
NATIONAL PARK

SANGAY NATIONAL PARK

LOCATION

Situated in the Cordillera Oriental region of the Andesin central Ecuador, covering parts of Morono Santiago,Chimborazo and Tungurahua provinces.
S 01° 27' to 02° 15', W 78° 04' to 78° 31'.

AREA

671,655ac (271,925ha).

FLORA

• The rainforest canopy reaches heights of 131ft (40m),with the lower stratas made up of micona and ferns.There are dense sections of cedro, aliso, and various palms, as well as wild avocado.

• Orchids flourish in the humid conditions and filtered sunlight, as do brilliantly colored wildflowers of the Gesneraceae and Lobeliaceae families.

• In the high country are cloud forest, grasslands, stands of bamboo and alpine rain tundra, with lichen petering out at the permanent snow line at 15,750ft (4,800m).

This lush national park, dominated by Sangay Volcano (16,863ft - 5,140m), which gives it its name, is made up of broad, alluvial fans which begin in the east and which turn into foothills - old, irregular mountains no higher than 6,600ft (2,000m) - before eventually mounting into the high country of the Andes. The older sections of the alluvial fans are sliced by deep canyons. The High Andes, which in Sangay represents the central and upper parts of the Cordillera Oriental, is rugged, splendid countryside, with sheer cliffs, knife-like peaks, glacial cirques and waterfalls in the 'hanging valleys' close to the edge of the Cordillera. The largest of the many lakes is Laguna Pintada. Six major rivers flow east towards the Amazon Basin, often overflowing their banks because of the region's high rainfall and steep grade. Their fluctuating water levels can cause serious erosion, which is only kept in check by the root systems of dense rainforest.

Although Sangay has many different types of forest, it is the rainforest which makes the most dramatic impression. The 'giants' can reach heights of up to 131ft (40m), and below their sheltering canopy are other stratas, made up of smaller trees, such as micona, and ferns. Orchids flourish in the humid conditions and filtered sunlight, and wildflowers of the gesneraceae and lobeliaceae families stand out in the shade with their astonishingly vibrant colors. Below 6,600ft (2,000m) can be found dense sections of cedro, aliso, and various palms, as well as wild avocado. Higher up there is cloud forest, grasslands, stands of bamboo and alpine rain tundra, its lichen petering out at the permanent snow line.

On the high ground can be found puma and Andean fox along with their prey: tapir and guinea pig; while further down on the slopes are spectacled bear; white-tailed deer; and giant otter. The wildcats can be found inside the rainforests: jaguar, ocelot and margay. There are an estimated 400 to 500 species of bird present in Sangay, the most famous also being the world's largest bird, the Condor, which is most often observed in the mountainous region of Altar, Cubillin and Quilimas. Cock-of-the-rock, a brightly colored orange-red bird which has an erect crest that can conceal its bill, and the world's largest humming bird, the giant humming bird, are two of the most notable species. Other remarkable birds include the torrent duck; the king vulture; and the swallow-tailed kite.

Before the coming of the Conquistadores in the early 16th Century, the region which is now the park was inhabited by around 30,000 Huamboya Indians, who were brutalized by the Spanish invaders, their numbers declining vertiginously due to murder, disease and ill-treatment. This of course has left a bitter and difficult legacy. Shuar Indians, who have been dispossessed of their traditional lands next to the park, must resort to illegal hunting inside Sangay in a constant struggle to survive. Although the park is virtually uninhabited (and hardly visited) due to its remoteness and difficulties of access, there are

- Among the many animals are Andean fox, tapir, guinea pig, spectacled bear, white-tailed deer, and giant otter.
- Wildcats include jaguar, puma, ocelot, and margay.
- There are an estimated 400 to 500 species of birds including the largest in the world, the condor, and the largest humming bird in the world, the giant humming bird. Other spectacular species are the cock-of-the-rock, the torrent duck, the swallow-tailed kite, and the king vulture.

FACILITIES

Because access into and around the park is so difficult, facilities are basic and not plentiful, and there are only about 1,000 visitors per year. Most concentrate on the Tungurahua Volcano area, or else practice mountaineering on the higher peaks of Tungurahua, El Altar, Cubillin, Quilimas and Sangay. The park's administrative headquarters is at Riobamba, and there are sentry posts set up at Aloa, San Isidro, Macas, Palora, Rio Negro, Candelaria, Atillo Purshi and Tungurahua.

(TOP LEFT)
King Vulture.

(LEFT)
Native Orchid.

about 400 inhabitants in the village of Atillo inside the park, who have had a number of clashes with park authorities, usually over illegal cultivation. Authorities are particularly worried about fires used to clear land getting out of control. In 1987 fires burnt 1,235ac (500ha) of land in Naranjal Chico and 2,470ac (1,000ha) of land in Atillo. The resulting loss in forest cover aggravates erosion, which in turn disrupts important watersheds.

One menace which could have dire consequences is the discovery of gold in the Llushin Grande and Huamboya regions. Not only might this lead to an enormous influx of prospectors, but could also slowly introduce mercury into the region's water supply. Gold prospectors in the Amazon, particularly in Brazil, use mercury when panning for gold, as the gold adheres readily to it. They then boil or burn the mercury, and after having extracted the gold, dump the mercury back into the waters. Although small quantities are used at a time, there have been so many prospectors

repeating the procedure so many times that there are now fears in Brazil that the country could be soon facing a mercury poisoning catastrophe. As a result of these various threats, Sangay has now been placed on the List of World Heritage in Danger.

TIKAL
NATIONAL PARK

Tikal National Park is an important transition zone from subtropical to tropical forest, with over 2,000 plant species present in the park. It also possesses a great wealth of animal life, with more than 300 birds, and a diverse selection of reptiles, insects and arthropods. Yet first and foremost, it is famous for one of the world's greatest and most astounding archeological sites. The quantity and quality of the finds in Tikal are extraordinary, with over 3,000 pre-Hispanic buildings dating from between 600BC to 900AD.

The structures found here, especially the temple complexes, are some of the greatest surviving relics of the Mayan Civilization. Buildings include private dwellings; public buildings such as ball-courts, squares, and ceremonial platforms; roads; palaces; and religious monuments-cum-tombs complete with involved hieroglyphic inscriptions. While archeological excavations have been able to reveal such things as the diet of the Mayans, which included seeds, beans, and fruit, and to note their progression from hunter-gatherers to agriculturalists with a written language, no real clues have emerged to satisfactorily explain what exactly happened to the Mayans which caused their civilization to 'vanish' apparently so quickly.

The ruins cover a relatively small section of the national park, occupying fairly level land that ranges up to 820ft (250m). Although the soil is poor, the vegetation is dense, thriving in the region's high humidity, sunshine and rainfall, with up to 80in (2,000mm) falling in the wet season, from September to February. Amongst the trees found in Tikal are cedar; West Indian mahogany; and bread-nut tree. There are many types of palm trees, most common being the palm Sabal mayarum, as well as orchids and ferns.

The park is a well-known site for viewing jungle animals, especially the howler monkey and the spider monkey, large numbers of both often congregating around the least visited of the Mayan

ruins, and in a section of the park prosaically called 'El Mondo Perdito', or 'the lost world'. There are several animals typical of Central America which can be glimpsed with relative ease in Tikal. The brown coati, a relative of the racoon with a slender body, long, ringed tail and an elongated snout, travels in groups, particularly when hunting for food such as iguana, and has a reputation for being a noisy, restless, curious creature.

Another relative of the racoon found in Tikal is the Kinkajou, a cat-sized animal covered with a short, wooly coat of fur, with a long tail and eyes reputed to reveal both intelligence and humor which, along with its friendly disposition, accounts for its popularity as a pet. Much more difficult to sight, but more famous than either the coati or the kinkajou, is the three-toed sloth, a mainly nocturnal, arboreal mammal celebrated for its lackadaisical ways.

Other typical animals found here are both the giant and the lesser anteaters, as well as the rarer dwarf anteater; the nine-banded armadillo; the long-tailed weasel and its cousin, the tayra; Baird's tapir; and both the white-lipped and collared peccary. Wild cats, such as the puma, margay, ocelot, and rarest and most powerful of all, the jaguar, should all be treated with caution.

Among the 303 species of birds frequenting the park, which represent 63 of the 74 families found in Guatemala, are the threatened El Peten turkey and three species of toucan. Tikal also has several species of both crocodile and turtle as well as many snakes, including the poisonous coral snake and two sub-species of rattlesnake. There are many types of spider.

Since the re-discovery of the Mayan Ruins, a lot of archeological work has been conducted and much excavation remains to be done. While this will have some inevitable effect on the national park's wildlife, what has caused far more disruption is the emergence of Guatemala as a popular tourist attraction, particularly for Europeans during their summer vacation. At the moment the lack of infrastructure at the site and the tenuous political situation in the country has meant that most tourists visit Tikal on day trips. Their increased presence has resulted in a far greater incidence of theft at the site. Some illegal poaching is also a problem.

in Guatemala, are the threatened el peten turkey and three species of toucan.

FACILITIES

There is an airport at the town of Flores, from where buses can be taken to the site, but these are infrequent. Accommodation and camping are available but can be over-booked in December and July and August. Visitors to the site should wear a hat and take water, which is sometimes not readily available. The Great Jaguar staircase in the Temple 1 complex should be negotiated with extreme caution, particularly when descending it.

(ABOVE) Nine-banded armadillo.

(FAR LEFT) Baird's tapir.

RIO PLATANO
BIOSPHERE RESERVE

RIO PLATANO BIOSPHERE RESERVE

LOCATION

In the departments of Gracias Adios, Colon and Olancho and partly in the isolated Mosquitia region, bordering the Caribbean in the north, N 15 ° 50′, W 84 ° 30′ to 85 ° 30′.

AREA

880sqmi (2,250sqkm).

FEATURES

This is one of the largest contiguous expanses of wildland in Central America and the largest surviving area of virgin tropical rainforest in Honduras.

FLORA

- Over 90% of the reserve is humid tropical forest.
- Vegetation types include pine savannas, mangroves, swamp forest fringing the coastal lagoons, and hardwood gallery forest along the Platano river and major tributaries.
- The greatest portion of the watershed is blanketed by mature broadleaf forest. The flora is not well known, but some 300 species have been identified.

This is one of the largest contiguous expanses of wildland in Central America and the largest surviving area of virgin tropical rainforest in Honduras. A steep, mountainous region, the dangers of stripping this land of its native vegetation has been well illustrated by the disastrous effects of soil erosion in the Patuca river basin, a result of thoughtless clearing for cultivation. We should all be clear on this point: any tampering with these finely balanced ecosystems will take this reserve down the road that has been chosen for so many similar areas before it - that of destruction.

The Rio Platano Biosphere Reserve is unusual in that it has been continuously inhabited since colonial times by 2,000 or so members of two indigenous groups - the Miskitos, the predominant group, and the Payas, who are believed by some ethnologists to be related to the Mayans. These people occupy only a small area of the park, subsisting on agriculture and hunting. The area of the reserve which is cultivated is confined to the mouth of the Platano River, upstream to the village of Batiltuk Las Marias, and the buffer zone. Unfortunately, one of the most immediate problems facing the park is posed by the Nicaraguan plan to resettle about 4,000 Miskito Indians on the border of the reserve's buffer zone. It is feared that the Miskitos will rapidly spill over into the reserve.

There are some valuable archeological sites in the park, most notably the fabled Ciudad Blanca, or 'White City' - one of the most important archeological sites of Mayan civilization. Other archeological remains include the Piedras Pintadas petroglyphs on the bed of the Platano River, believed to belong to an unknown pre-Columbian culture. The reserve also contains the site where Christopher Colombus discovered the Americas in 1492.

The reserve protects virtually the entire watershed of the 60mi (100km) long Platano River, as well as major portions of the Paulaya, Guampu and Sicre Rivers. These three waterways and the Caribbean form the boundaries. The rugged mountainous headwaters encompass almost 75% of the reserve, rising to Punta Piedra at 4,350ft (1,326m), coastal plains comprise the remainder. The mountainous peaks of this park are some of the most magnificent in Latin America, particularly spectacular is the rocky, 'finger shaped' formation known as 'El Viejo', and 'Pico Dama', which rises to a height of 500ft (150m) from a mountain peak. From the highest peak, Mt Cuyamel or Mirador, there is a waterfall starting from perhaps the greatest height in Central America. The vegetation on the peaks is limited to only a few species. In the rest of the forest there is a great variety but there

(LEFT) The Platano River.

has been so little research done in the reserve that the extent and number of species which it contains is not really known. Amongst the species of plants known to need protection are native cedar and mahogany.

The lower river area is mostly low plains interspersed with swamps. It has poor soil and mainly grows Yagua palm, pine, and grasses. The Platano river is approximately 66mi (100km) long and averages 100ft (30m) in width. It possesses many rapids, the most turbulent of which, the 'subterraneo', is 1mi (1.5km) long, and takes two days to negotiate in the dry season. There is a small patch of degraded secondary forest on the river bank which is used for cultivation but for the most part the banks are now left alone and the regrowth is quite advanced. Navigation by water is the main means of transport in the area, there are two small runways and only a few footpaths.

The buffer zone contains the Paulaya and Lagarto river basins and borders onto Ebano and Brus lagoons, both of which are polluted. The Brus lagoon which is approximately 47sqmi (120sqkm) and surrounded by mangroves and coconut palms, is fed by the Patuca river which is polluted by sediment resulting from poor land management in

the basin area and by human waste from the local population.

There is an enormous variety of animal life in the forests, of mammals, amphibians and reptiles, fish, and birds. Endangered mammals include the Central American tapir, the panther, and the Southern river otter. Amongst the reptiles there is the American crocodile and the iguana. The 'cuyamel' fish (joturus pichardi) is much sought after which has caused problems with outsiders fishing illicitly in the dry season. The fishing of the local inhabitants offers no great threat but measures have had to be taken to restrict visitors from overfishing the rivers. Many birds inhabit the reserve area and some such as the harpy eagle and the red macaw are endangered.

The area of the reserve under greatest threat is in the south. A special operational plan with funding support from WWF-US and UNESCO was put into effect in 1988. Refugees displaced by the war in Nicaragua and by industrial logging operations outside the reserve, were relocated outside the reserve, where they previously had sought sanctuary. Sawmill operations and road

construction within the buffer zone were halted. Uncontrolled resource use, mainly in the southern headwaters of the watershed, from improper logging practices, slash and burn agriculture and deforestation to promote cattle grazing have resulted in an emergency in the reserve management. Other threats include illegal hunting, plundering of archeological remains and potential timber exploitation. There are plans to build a road from the Department of Olancho to the political center of Puerto Lempira, which will pass close to the southern border of the reserve and increase the danger of unplanned, detrimental colonization.

(ABOVE) Caiman.

(FAR LEFT) Military macaw.

(LEFT) Crested guan.

DARIÉN
NATIONAL PARK

DARIÉN
NATIONAL PARK

LOCATION

The park is located in the province of Darién to the east of Santa Fe and the Gulf of San Miguel, and covers the region adjacent to the Colombian border, N 07° 12' to 08° 31', W 77° 09' to 78° 25'.

AREA

1,380,000ac (575,000ha).

FEATURES

Darién is remarkable for its varied terrain which, although it extends over a relatively small area, has given rise to what is considered the most diverse ecosystem in Central America, with large areas of both primary and secondary forest.

FLORA

- Within its monsoon forest, the average height of the trees in the top layer is 130ft (40m), with some individual specimens reaching up to 165ft (50m).
- In the lowlands are freshwater marshes, mangrove and palm forest swamps.

FAUNA

- Crocodiles and caimans have sought refuge here.
- Many types of monkey are to be found in the forests, including the douroucoulis, the brown-headed spider monkey; and the howler monkey.

Darién National Park is located in the southern part of Panama in Darién Province, its 1,380,000ac (575,000ha) lying between the Serrania del Darién, near the Caribbean Sea, and the Pacific Ocean. As Panama is the bridge between the Americas, and as the national park runs along 80% of the border with Colombia, it occupies a strategic position between the Southern and Northern Hemispheres. It can only be hoped that political sensitivities will not present a future threat to this area, which along with Colombia's contiguous Los Katios National Park, is the largest surviving lowland tropical forest on the Pacific coast in all of Central America.

Darién is remarkable for its varied terrain which, although it extends over a relatively small area, has given rise to what is considered the most diverse ecosystem in Central America, with large areas of both primary and secondary forest. Within its monsoon forest, the average height of the trees in the top layer is 130ft (40m), with some individual specimens reaching up to 165ft (50m).

As well as the multifarious, stratified society so typical of rainforest, Darién is noteworthy for its twice daily tides from the Pacific. These big Pacific tides, ranging up to over 20ft (6m), control the levels of the Tuira and Chucunaque rivers for many miles inland. This tidal activity has engendered large areas of wetland forests, where there are significant stands of 'cativo', the most common timber tree of the region, which reaches heights of up to 100ft (30m). Also in the lowlands are freshwater marshes, mangrove and palm forest swamps, and extensive sandy beaches along an often craggy coast. Shifting away from the sea towards the mountains in the east, the lowland tropical forest gives way, above 660ft (200m), to cloud forest and elfin forest.

As could be expected, given the extent of the wetlands, crocodiles and caimans have sought refuge here. Both are threatened. Many types of monkey found in the forests, including the douroucoulis, a small, nocturnal monkey with large, round eyes which resemble an owl's; the brown-headed spider monkey; and the howler monkey. Also present are the giant anteater; the jaguar and its smaller cousin, the ocelot; the tapir and its cousin, the peccary; and the agoutis, a small, short-eared rodent.

Inside Darién National Park live two indigenous peoples: the Chocoe Indians, who number about 1,000, and the Cunas, who number only around 200. Both groups were living here when Columbus explored the coastline in 1502, and they suffered at the hands of roving Conquistadores and then Spanish settlers, who introduced slavery before abandoning the area at the beginning of the eighteenth century. Today the two tribes possess 10% of the park's area, which they use for traditional agricultural pursuits. After centuries of abuse, the park authorities were careful to make maintaining the traditions and culture of the Cunas and Chocoe peoples a priority of the park's overall conservation management strategy. Although the rest of the land within Darién is supposedly owned by the state, in fact there are segments in the west which are occupied illegally by small farmers. Though not a real danger to the park at the moment, their presence is a menace in that it establishes a precedent, especially if, as some fear, this southern region of Panama is overrun with newly-arrived settlers.

Such settlers would come from two different directions. Panamanians from the north are attracted to the south of the country because of its extremely low population: the province of Darién, although accounting for 22% of Panama's land, is home to a mere 1.6% of the national population. The threat from the south involves a proposal that the 'Carretera Panamericana' or Pan American Highway be extended through the national park. At the moment, Darién represents the only section of the region where the highway does not run. If the arguments for the completion of the highway prevail, there will in all probability be a rush for land, particularly near the border with Colombia. This would see more sections of the park seized by illegal farmers; some degree of poaching; and almost certainly a disruption to the indigenous peoples' way of life. The highway would also allow illegal loggers to penetrate the forests and to quickly ship their timber out. Darién is the most extensively protected area in all of Central America because of the fragility of its ecosystem. Any disruption to that protection will inevitably be disastrous. A decision on the building of the highway will probably be taken shortly. In the meantime, Colombia's nomination of the adjacent

Los Katios National Park as a World Heritage Site will probably make it a little easier to reject the highway.

While there are no tourist facilities at the moment, plans exist for a tourist development zone of some 19,200ac (8,000ha), which would enable visitors to study some of the endemic flora and fauna whilst not disturbing the indigenous peoples, whose traditional lands would be designated a cultural zone. There is an administrative area in Yaviza, close to the park, which is used by rangers, together with a hotel, a hospital and a tuberculosis clinic and the nearby towns of El Real and Boca de Cupe (both home to many of those illegally farming park lands) offer rudimentary lodging with families.

FACILITIES

Access into the park is very difficult, and the best approach is by bus to Yaviza, and then by boat to El Real, and dugout canoe to Boca de Cupe. The coast can be approached by private craft, but permission should be sought in advance. If the Pan American Highway is extended through the park, the ease of access will become a major problem.

(ABOVE LEFT) Capybara.

(BOTTOM LEFT) Squirrel monkey.

(FAR LEFT) Giant anteater.

HUASCARÁN
NATIONAL PARK

HUASCARÁN NATIONAL PARK

LOCATION

Located in the Cordillera Blanca, in the Sierra Central of Peru in the Department of Ancash in the Andes, S 08° 50' to 10° 40', W 77° 07' to 77° 49'.

AREA

816,000ac (340,000ha).

FEATURES

This the home of the highest altitude tropical rainforest in the world. Lining the lower peaks and mountain sides, just beneath the rugged white-capped peaks, is a belt of wild humid montane forest.

FLORA

Some 120 species of plants have been identified, including endemic alpine bromeliads, together with other bromeliad species, mountain orchids and patches of ancient relict forests.

FAUNA

- Most notable of the surviving mammals are the spectacled bear, puma, mountain cat, North Andean huemul, white-tailed deer, and vicuna.
- The birdlife is rich and includes the Andean condor, Gurney's buzard, giant humingbird, giant coot and ornate tinamou.

(RIGHT) Andean condor.

Rugged and largely inaccessible, the steep sided valleys and ridges of this reserve provide magnificent views of glaciers and lakes perched on richly forested mountain slopes, where icy waters rush down steep ravines. The occasional thunderous tremor sends tons of rocky debris on its way down these peaceful valleys, releasing plumes of snow and ice into the crackling air. Thermal springs gurgle below, spilling into warm streams lined with ferns and mosses.

This reserve sits atop the mighty Cordillera Blanca, part of the prodigious Andean mountain chain. El Huascarán, at 22,300ft (6,768m) is the highest peak in the Cordillera Blanca, and the highest peak in the Andes. This range boasts 27 snow-capped peaks, 30 glaciers and 120 glacial lakes, some holding up to 109 million cubic feet (10 million cubic meters) of water.

This is the home of the highest altitude tropical rainforest in the world. Lining the lower peaks and mountain sides, just beneath the rugged white-capped peaks, is a belt of wild humid montane forest. The contrast between the deep, rich green hues of the rainforest and the icy blue world of the peaks is almost surreal.

Living in this otherworldly landscape, are some very distinctive species. Some 120 species of plants have been identified, including endemic alpine bromeliads, together with other Bromeliaceae species, mountain orchids and patches of ancient relict forests.

Much of the mammal population has suffered badly at the hands of hunters and poachers. The improved access to the area which would result from the proposal to construct a road linking the Callejon de Huayalas in the east and the Callejon de Canchucas could aggravate this problem. Most notable of the surviving mammals are the spectacled bear, puma, mountain cat, North Andean huemul, white-tailed deer, and vicuna. The birdlife is rich and includes the Andean condor, Gurney's buzard, giant humingbird, giant coot and ornate tinamou.

There are pre-Inca ruins in the park, belonging to the Huarus and Huaylas people. These ancient dwellings have been ransacked for their treasures but still maintain an awe-inspiring dignity and beauty, as well as being of immense archeological interest. Despite its rugged topography and extreme temperatures (often as low as 92°F - 30°C) the area has not escaped human interference. The main changes have been caused by the ravages of fires started both by careless tourists, and by those clearing neighboring land for pasture; as well as by ice collection from the glaciers, and, to a lesser extent, careless littering by mountaineering expeditions.

FACILITIES

The park is popular with mountaineers and there is a well developed system of trekking and mountaineering routes - the largest concentration in Peru. There is a small visitor center, hostel and campsite.

(LEFT) Puya raimondii, *a distinctive alpine bromeliad.*

MACHU PICCHU
NATIONAL PARK

MACHU PICCHU
NATIONAL PARK

LOCATION

The site is located on the highest part of the eastern highlands of the Andes, above the Rio Urubamba northwest of Cuzco,
S 13° 10′ to 13° 13′,
W 72° 33′ to 72° 37′.

AREA

78,220ac (32,592ha).

FEATURES

This park was established to protect the natural heritage and landscape of the region around the ancient ruins of Machu Picchu.

FLORA

• The remnant areas of untouched forest range from dry and sub-tropical to humid low montane and harbor species such as mahogany, lauraceae and the only Peruvian conifer podocarpus.

• There is a variety of tree ferns and palms.

FAUNA

• Some interesting mammals inhabit the forests, including dwarf brocket deer, long-tailed weasel, pampas cat, and ocelot.

• Of particular importance is the spectacled bear.

(ABOVE RIGHT)
A male kestral.

This park was established to protect the natural heritage and landscape of the region around the ancient ruins of Machu Picchu. It is situated in the eastern highlands of the Andes plateau, where a shattered, cracked and eroded massif rises steeply out of the fertile alluvial basin of the Uramba River valley.

The mountains are an interesting geological mosaic with a combination of volcanic material, intrusive rocks, marine and sedimentary rocks including schists slates and quartzites. There is a thin covering of soil, only able to support grasses and herbaceous shrubs. The Incas did their best to deal with this obstacle to cultivation by modifying the mountainside. The remnants of a complex system of terraces is clearly evident today.

Around the magnificent ruins of the 'lost city', paramo grassland is dominant but patches of bamboo can also be found. The ruins themselves, elaborate collections of stone walls, paved roads and stairways believed to have been the summer palace of the 'sapa Inca' - the Incan King as incarnation of the Sun God - are covered with a rich layer of grass. The Incan city, perched high above the valley and near to the sun was built in the perfect position for such a noble purpose as harboring the Sun King's palace.

The site has magnificent views of the surrounding area including the beautiful Vilcanota valley and the verdant and rocky cloud-wreathed massifs that surround it. The sharp lines of the ridges and the contrast of grey-white cliffs against the dark green foliage is softened by an ever present mist.

Numerous species of birds live in the higher altitudes. Andean vulture and Andean cock-of-the-rock live on the ridges whilst black-tailed train-bearer, white-winged black-tyrant, tufted tit tyrant, cinereous conebill, blue-capped tanage and rufus-collared sparrow haunt the ruins. Particular to the bamboo thickets which characterize the ridges, is the wren species *Thryothorus*..

The area boasts numerous streams and rivers edged by reeds and sometimes by willow and alder.

Along these streams can be found the occasional otter as well as torrent duck, white-capped dipper, fasciated tiger-heron and numerous frogs and lizards. The waterways of the park carry water down into the river valleys, carving deeply into the soil until they join major rivers and streams, many of which end up in the Amazon.

The Incas may have been some of the earliest peoples to change the face of this landscape, but they were far from being the last. Much of the land has been affected by human changes so that the park incorporates man-made habitats, partially degraded forest and areas of regrowth where cultivation has previously occurred. Burning to clear for agriculture is still a problem, as are accidental fires. Both have caused an enormous amount of damage to the environment. The remnant areas of untouched forest range from dry and sub-tropical to humid low montane. They harbor species such as mahogany, lauraceae and the only Peruvian conifer *podocarpus*. There is a variety of tree ferns and palms. Some interesting mammals inhabit these forests, including dwarf brocket deer, long-tailed weasel, pampas cat, and ocelot. Of particular importance is the spectacled bear. According to Inca legend this bear is the messenger between the spirits of the jungle and those of the mountain peaks, just as the mountains themselves are the pathways from the earth to the heavens. Although the population of bear in the park is not large enough to be self-sustaining the park is an important corridor joining populations in the oriental and central ranges.

with Chachapoyas to the north, crosses the western boundary of the park and archeological sites have been found throughout the zone of influence of this route. The ruins, including roads, shelters, dwellings and ceremonial sites, span 8,000 years of Peruvian history and prehistory and provide an important and fascinating view of earlier civilizations. The number and variety of archeological sites indicate a significant level of human occupation in the past.

Unfortunately, the all to common stories of illegal hunting, slash and burn agriculture, logging and road encroachment have been reported in Rio Abiseo. There are many positive signs though, since the park was closed to the public and a park administrator began work in 1986, steps have been taken to protect the integrity of this most important treasure. Illegal hunting is regarded as uncommon today; burning of pastures is diminishing, although it continues to be a medium to serious threat in the high elevations of the western sector of the park; timber harvesting is now regarded as not a grave threat, but habitat destruction on the steep slopes is still being reported. Park guards are being trained to work

with inhabitants of neighbouring communities on the appropriate use of renewable natural resources. The efforts of the Peruvian Environmental Law Society and park personnel have led to some graziers exchanging their cattle for alpacas, an animal which is ecologically less damaging to the local environment and whose grazing habits do not necessitate the periodic harmful burning of grasslands.

• Invertebrates boast a particularly high number of endemic species.

FACILITIES

Due to the fragility of the archeological ruins and the lack of park infrastructure, Rio Abiseo has not been open to tourism since 1986 Since public use is significantly restricted, the park is classified more as a strictly scientific reserve than a national park. The local authorities have given permission to improve tourist facilities ranging from the construction of a road from Juanjui-Dos to Mayo-Gran Pajaten to the planned development of a tourist hotel at Juanjui, and a museum at Huicungo. As yet the projects have not advanced beyond the planning stage due to a lack of funding The international division of the US National Park Service has offered the services of a trail specialist, when funding becomes available to construct and mark trails and establish camp sites.

(TOP LEFT) Jaguar.

(BOTTOM LEFT) Peruvian cock of the rock.

NEW WORLD HERITAGE PARKS

The following six sites were nominated at the end of 1993 for inclusion on the World Heritage List and are likely to be accepted for 1995.

AFRICA

UGANDA
Rwenzori Mountains National Park

LOCATION
On the border between Uganda and Zaire, largely within the Western Rift valley,
N 00°06' to 00°46', E 29°47' to 30°11'.

AREA
240,000ac (99,600ha): contiguous in the east with Virunga National Park in Zaire, already a World Heritage site.

FLORA
• The Rwenzori are well known for their unusual flora which includes many species endemic to the Albertine Rift in the higher altitude zones. Most stunning are the giant heathers, groundsels, ericas and lobelias of the tree heath and alpine zones.

• The montane forest zone merges into a bamboo forest zone, which occurs in pure stands in many places up to an altitude of 10,000ft (3,000m).

FAUNA
• The mountains contain at least 89 species of forest bird (27% of the country's total), 4 species of diurnal primate, and 15 species of butterfly (22% of the country's total)

• A high level of sub-specific endemism occurs, including the Rwenzori colobus monkey, hyrax and leopard.

• A recent study of invertebrate life forms listed 60 species in the alpine zone, 25 of which are new to science. This is indicative of a much more extensive fauna waiting to be discovered.

• Although in low numbers, the following globally threatened species are found in the park: African elephant, chimpanzee and l'hoests monkey.

FACILITIES
There are no facilities within this park; access is extremely difficult and often dangerous.

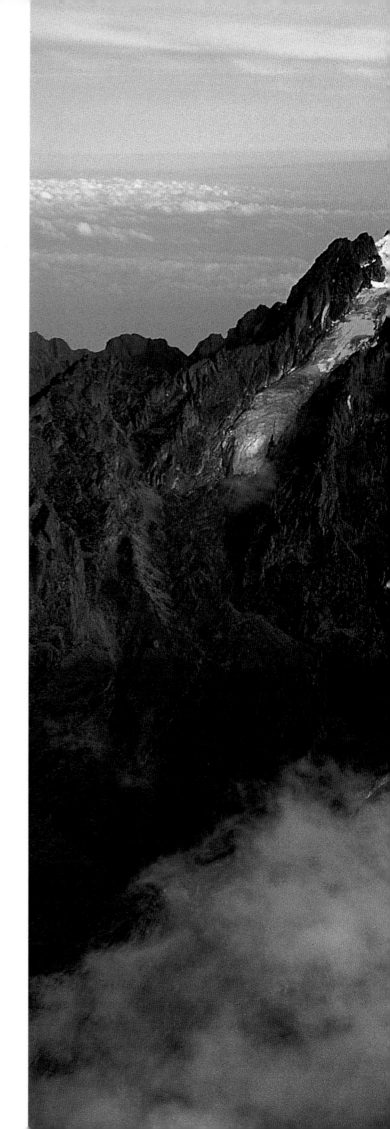